Of Heretics, Traitors and True Believers

The War for the Soul of Williamsburg

Published by Telford Publications*

Design by Andrew Evans Design
Illustrations by David Eccles

© George T. Morrow II 2011

Telford Publications
301 Mill Stream Way,
Williamsburg, VA, U.S.A., 23185

Tel (757) 565-7215
Fax (757) 565-7216
www.williamsburgincharacter.com

FIRST EDITION

Telford Publications is named for Alexander Telford,
a volunteer rifleman from Rockbridge County, Virginia, who
served in three Revolutionary War campaigns, in the last of which,
Yorktown, he was personally recognized by Gen. George Washington
for his extraordinary marksmanship with the long rifle.

ISBN 978-0-9831468-4-1
Printed and bound by Sheridan Press, 450 Fame Avenue, Hanover, PA

Of Heretics, Traitors and True Believers

The War for the Soul of Williamsburg

George T. Morrow II

WILLIAMSBURG IN CHARACTER

Bruton Parish Church
"The forced intimacy was hard to bear"

To Joan

"If a man could say nothing against a character but what he can prove, history could not be written."

SAMUEL JOHNSON

Contents

List of Illustrations

Preface

The adjective parochial, both in its straightforward and its dismissive sense, might have been coined especially to describe the clash between the Rev. Samuel Henley and Robert Carter Nicholas over the rectorate of Bruton Church in Williamsburg. But as George Morrow vividly recounts here, it was about so much more than a single clerical appointment, turning out to be one of the paving stones on the path the colony of Virginia took towards revolution. The heresies that Nicholas discovered in Henley, brought out into the open in 1773 at the vestry meeting to decide whether to appoint him rector, triggered doubts and suspicions in Nicholas's mind. And these were soon not confined to the Church of England but spread to the state of the British Constitution, with special reference to the Thirteen Colonies. Suddenly and unexpectedly this conventional, conservative, unprepossessing member of the Virginia establishment was turned into one of the most effective voices crying defiance in the face of the ministers of George III.

On the last page of his essay Morrow says that Nicholas "did not wish to desert the English church and constitution: he wished to defend and affirm them." This apparent paradox and central fact can perhaps be seen more clearly from a British historical perspective. Here was not some surprise intellectual somersault that Nicholas was performing – he had not reversed the normal direction of travel in men's lives, from the political left to the right. The conventional belief to which he firmly subscribed was that the English church and state were indissolubly linked together, that any diminution of the former weakened the latter. The full panoply of the Divine Right of Kings might have been considerably tempered since the time of James I and Charles I, but there was still what has been called a "dynastic political theology" about: George III was still the Head of the Church of England and, along with many of his subjects including Nicholas, would have agreed with James I's cry of "No Bishop, No King," meaning that the introduction of a Presbyterian church system would lead to the end of monarchy. Given that church and state were joined at the hip, to have discovered as rotten an apple – to mix metaphors – in the Church of England barrel, as Henley so obviously and unashamedly was, had to set Nicholas wondering whether the British Constitution, was not in danger too. When he came to write his *Strictures* against Attorney-General John Randolph, about Randolph's attack on the rights of subjects and about what had been going on in Boston, he did not talk in terms of new measures or initiatives but of a return to the old, immemorial ways, a restoration not a revolution.

It was the Administration in London that was revolutionary, acting as Nicholas said and as George Morrow quotes, "contrary to every Principle of Law and Justice . . . utterly subversive of everything dear and valuable." In appealing for a return to the past Nicholas was only following in the footsteps of the radicals before and during the English Civil War a hundred and more years before. They had constantly appealed to the Magna Carta of 1215 and insistently claimed that the despotic rule of William the Conqueror and his successors in the preceding centuries – The Norman Yoke – was an aberration. Before that there had been rule by the assemblages, the Moots and Witans of Anglo-Saxon days, whose traditions had then gone underground, only to re-emerge in the early parliaments of the 13th century and in England's Common Law.

Nicholas did not spell out in this way what lay behind his stance, but when Thomas Jefferson wrote his *Summary View of the Rights of the British in America* in July 1774, he did. The *Summary*, meant for the guidance of Virginia's first delegation to the Continental Congress, though too radical for the delegation's tastes, was what first drew the attention of a wider world to this young lawyer, foreshadowing as it did the cutting clarity of the Declaration of Independence. Jefferson, applying what later was known as the Whig Interpretation, discounted all English history since the arrival of the Normans in 1066 and appealed instead to some pristine, arcadian, proto-democratic, Saxon past as the justification for denying either George III or the Parliament in Westminster any jurisdiction in America.

Compared to these heavyweight matters, the heterodox opinions of Samuel Henley do not register high on the scale, but the background to them, how they could emerge and then survive within the Church of England, is intriguing. A good portion of the "C of E" in the 18th century, adopting the prevailing rational, scientific outlook of the Enlightenment, found its evidence for the Hand of God by exercising its powers of observation throughout Nature, rather than taking it from the revelations set out in the Bible. Here was a grand design minutely worked out, moving like a piece of clockwork; once set in motion, further divine intervention was not to be expected. Past miracles could be accepted, but they were surplus to requirements in the predictable, ordered present. God, the clockmaker, had withdrawn into the distance; natural, rational religion had replaced the supernatural and the emotional, and the sacraments were administered infrequently. It was what the economist Max Weber called the "disenchantment of the world." Some members of the C of E however, and some Dissenters outside it, were not prepared to stop there. They went under various names and strayed different distances beyond the confines of the C of E's 39 Articles. Deists stayed closest, though with dubious views on the Trinity and the after-life. For example, Governor Fauquier of Virginia had been suspected of holding Deist views. Arians held that Jesus, though divine, was not co-equal with but created by God the Father. For Socinians, Jesus was not divine, merely a moral exemplar. This meant no doctrine of mankind's atonement via the Cross, so no original sin, and that there could be no priesthood divinely instituted by Jesus and then descending via the Apostolic Succession. Once more, the cry of "No Bishop, No King" might be heard.

How, it might be asked, were Socinians allowed inside the C of E? It was because the Whig oligarchy of the years 1714 to 1760 were reluctant to prosecute, and thus give any weapons to their orthodox Tory foes. The most infamous Socinian of the day was Bishop Benjamin Hoadly of Bangor. When he cast doubt on the C of E's claims to the Apostolic Succession in 1717, the Administration was even prepared to suspend Convocation, the Church's advisory assembly, indefinitely to avoid controversy. Popular at Court, and an especial favourite of George III's queen, Caroline, Hoadly was promoted to be Bishop of Hereford, then Salisbury, then Winchester. Queen Caroline reputedly said that the only objection to making this good Whig Archbishop of Canterbury was that "he was not a Christian." When the Rev. Thomas Gwatkin went into print at Williamsburg in support of his friend Henley against Nicholas in 1772, using the pseudonym Hoadleianus, that should have set off alarm bells among orthodox church members. John Butler, who became Bishop of Oxford in 1777, was asked by his patron the politician Lord Onslow to write a defence of the 39 Articles when they were under attack in 1772. Butler, who had subscribed to them 30 years before, when he became a beneficed clergyman, reported that they were tolerable, "without trying your patience by reading them." This must have been Henley's attitude after, as mentioned by George Morrow, he came under the influence of the group of Socinians in Cambridge University revolving round Edmund Law, Master of Peterhouse there, and non-resident Bishop of Carlisle to boot. This last position Law owed to the Duke of Grafton, George Ill's first minister for a short period and of a similar religious persuasion to Law. Before he entered the Peterhouse circle the 39 Articles had been no concern of Henley's since he was a Dissenter, outside the C of E.

Henley was a man with no expectations and his way to make in the world and, as George Morrow points out, his career path suggests strongly that he was none too scrupulous in how he achieved advancement. Nicholas thwarted him in 1773. The lives of two other members of the Peterhouse circle, John Jebb and Capel Lofft, suggest that he might then have thrown in his lot with the American rebels. Jebb, to whom Henley dedicated the printed version of his sermon attacking Nicholas's proposal for regulating dissenters in Virginia, left the church, disgusted by the failure in 1772 of what was called the Feathers Tavern Petition, to get Parliament to abolish subscription to the 39 Articles as a requirement for C of E clergymen. He became a doctor and Lofft a lawyer before transforming themselves into political radicals, champions of the American Revolution and leading members of the Society for Constitutional Information. This was set up in London in 1780 to press for the full democratic package: manhood suffrage, annual parliaments, secret ballots, etc. To have done something similarly principled in Virginia was, one suspects, too high-risk an option to appeal to Henley. As George Morrow tells us in fascinating detail, he instead chose a more exotic route, first attaching himself to a ducal house and then mixing in with one of the most scandalous and eccentric figures to be found in the latter days of Georgian England, William Beckford: traveller, writer, bisexual, aesthete, recluse, and builder of Fonthill Abbey, the greatest folly ever raised in England.

What followed was Henley's connivance, if that is what it was, in the goings-on at Fonthill at Christmas in 1781, his passing off the English translation of Beckford's *Vathek* as entirely his own and publishing it against the express wishes of Beckford, and finally his inglorious and very undistinguished time as head of the new East India College. This is some indictment, and perhaps one should look to see if anything can be rescued from it. Tim Mowl, Beckford's most recent biographer, has read Beckford's original French version of *Vathek* and says that it is often clumsy and convoluted, but that some of the additions and alterations suggested by Henley are equally inept. Yet the English version that finally emerged from their collaboration has long been accepted as a minor yet influential classic, one of the very few pieces of English fiction of any quality to appear between the novels of Smollett and those of Jane Austen. Henley also had a large editorial role in Beckford's very original accounts of his Continental travels, now known under the title *Dreams, Waking Thoughts and Incidents*. Maybe there is a case for seeing theirs as a truly creative collaboration: by themselves neither was a writer of much merit, but what they produced working together was often outstanding.

As for the East India College at Hertford, it was a remarkable new venture set up to provide a specialised training for youths before they went out to become officials administering Britain's possessions in India. They were taught a minimum of three oriental languages: Sanskrit, Persian – the official language of the old Moghul Empire in India – and Hindustani. On top of that they studied classical languages, mathematics, law, history and political economy, this last hardly touched in the older universities. Henley may have contributed little or nothing to the originality of its curriculum or to its achieve-ment, but we can at least attribute benign neglect to him: he may not have helped as he should, but he did not hinder either.

There is some sort of ironic symmetry to the fact that he first came to attention in the North American colonies, the centre-piece of Britain's early Empire, and then bowed out in the service of India, by far the most important part of her later Empire.

ROGER HUDSON,
LONDON

Of Heretics, Traitors and True Believers

The War for the Soul of Williamsburg

It may be relied on as a certain Truth,
exemplified by the most extensive Experience,
that no Man can be safely trusted, who does not
act upon *solid, virtuous* Principles.[1]

> Robert Carter Nicholas, 1774,
> *Strictures on the Attorney*
> *General's Plea for Moderation*

The weather in Virginia on June 11, 1773 was terrible. At Mount Vernon, snow and an "exceeding cold," fresh wind from the Northwest kept even George Washington indoors. In Williamsburg, Thomas Jefferson, who had just lost "the dearest friend [he] possessed on earth," his brother-in-law, Dabney Carr, spent most of the day selling old law books in an effort to pay his debts.[2]

Jefferson's first sale, which raised £22, was to John Tazewell, a rising lawyer whose practice was mostly centered on James City County Courthouse in Market Square.[3] His second, for £20, was to "a young man studying law under Mr. [Benjamin] Waller." From Waller's house near the capitol, Jefferson then made the rounds of Williamsburg, paying out money to friends, inlaws, even a ferryboat owner: a total of eleven transactions in 24 hours. One of his last stops was at the Market Square home of Virginia Treasurer Robert Carter Nicholas. There, Jefferson paid Nicholas' wife, Ann Cary Nicholas, an unspecified amount, described in his Account Book simply as "for myself." If he saw the Treasurer, Jefferson failed to mention it; nor, as far as can be known, did he run into Nicholas at any other time during his 24 hours in the city.[4]

The omission (if that is what it was) represents something of a lost opportunity, both for Jefferson himself and for those interested in the history of the Revolution in Virginia. As a reader of the *Virginia Gazette*, Jefferson surely knew that Nicholas was involved in a bitter dispute with Rev. Samuel Henley over Henley's fitness to become rector of Bruton Parish Church. Nearly anyone in the city could have told Jefferson that Nicholas had charged Henley with heresy and that Henley was to be tried the following day, June 12, in the tower beneath the church steeple. In Virginia, church attendance was required by law. Heresy mattered. The fact that the alleged heretic was Professor of Moral Philosophy at the College of William and Mary also signified.

At the time, the trial of Rev. Henley by the vestry of Bruton Parish Church was viewed as a *cause célèbre*. These days, and despite Rhys Isaac's excellent analysis of the case in *The Transformation of Virginia* (1982), the name Robert Carter Nicholas is as unknown outside the Historic Area as that of Samuel Henley. There may be no anti-religious bias in histories of early America, but there is clearly a hierarchy of interest; and in a contest between war and revolution, esoteric religious controversies usually come in last.

In that respect, Thomas Jefferson must be considered quintessentially modern. As someone who privately viewed the idea of the Trinity as a "hocus-pocus Phantasm," Jefferson could be expected to have little interest in the English Church and perhaps even less in its controversies. In short, if it was a crime for Rev. Henley to call the Trinity "a persona," Jefferson was equally guilty.[5] This is not to say of course that Jefferson was ready to take sides in the dispute. As he later told his friend and former colleague at the bar, John Randolph, "There may be people to whose tempers and dispositions . . . contention is pleasing but to me it is of all states but one [i.e., death] the most horrid."[6]

Jefferson was not exaggerating. He dreaded conflict and this was likely to be an aggravated case. The parties were insisting on it. Henley thought his "moral Character" had been impugned. Predictably, his accuser felt the same way, though perhaps with less reason. Nor was this a controversy Jefferson could avoid by simply retreating to his aerie at Monticello. Henley was a friend, a scholar – a lover of the classics – albeit one with very different political views.[7] Henley's sponsors for the rector's job included Peyton Randolph, Jefferson's cousin on his mother's side, and George Wythe, with whom Jefferson had studied law at the College of William and Mary. On the other side of the dispute, Robert Carter Nicholas had administered Jefferson's bar exam. Just recently, he had offered to give Jefferson what was left of his once-extensive law practice.[8]

Yet, though Nicholas and Jefferson were brothers at the bar, they had little in common. Outside the church, Nicholas had few interests, while Jefferson's love of scientific speculation and casual neglect of his financial obligations effectively ensured that he and the Treasurer would never be friends.

Dr. Samuel Johnson would not have called Nicholas a club-bable man. He was dull. Even the Treasurer's best friends thought he was dull. It did not help that he was balding, short (this in an age when the average man was five-feet-six), deeply pious and at forty-six no longer young. Lord Dunmore would later compare Nicholas' "abilities as [a] lawyer . . . and [man] of integrity" to those of Peyton and John Randolph, describing them as "equal . . . to any . . . in the colony."[9] Evidently the Assembly was of the same mind, as it had conferred the title of

Treasurer on Nicholas. But that was in itself a reward for dullness and for taking on the Randolph interest when Peyton, in imitation of his predecessor, sought to combine the titles of Treasurer and Speaker of the House. The one thing about Nicholas that could not be called dull were his friends, including Arthur Lee, whose call to "hail his country free with his latest breath" (published in Rind's April 28, 1768 *Virginia Gazette*)[10] was clearly still ringing in the Treasurer's ears when he sat down a year later to give Lee an update on his current state of mind regarding American rights and liberties:

> You were fully acquainted with my Sentiments upon the grand affair [the ongoing dispute between England and America]: I still retain them in their utmost Vigour: I have always professed myself a friend to Decency and Moderation but at the same Time am as firmly attach'd and riveted to the Main Principle as any Man alive; my political Creed was published to the World in the different Applications to Government from our former Assembly, & I am as little inclined to depart one Jot or Tittle of it, that I would avow it with my latest Breath . . . [W]e honour and esteem our Governour, as the Representative of our gracious Sovereign & hope we shall continue to do so for his own good Qualities; he does what he thinks his Duty, & we what is ours.[11]

An avowed moderate, Nicholas could be ferocious if he felt his principles were endangered. Meanwhile, the current object of his esteem, Lord Botetourt, was becoming a personal role model, so dear to the Treasurer that he would name his second son after Botetourt's given name, Norborne. Could a firm Anglican and a patriot with good qualities achieve true happiness in 1770 Virginia? Under Gov. Botetourt it seemed that he could, as just six months after his letter to Lee, Nicholas again described Botetourt to Lee as a fine "Gentleman of the most enlarged and liberal sentiments," adding that, "We think ourselves extremely happy here in our Governour."[12] But what if this paragon should die? Would he find as many good qualities in his successor? And what if Nicholas' beloved church were to fall into the hands of a heretic? Nicholas – and Virginia – were about to find out.

Samuel Henley arrived in Virginia in the fall of 1770. He was then 25 years old, the *protege* of a friend of Lord Botetourt who had been asked by his Lordship to find the best qualified man in England to fill the job of Professor of Moral Philosophy at William and Mary. That Henley was clever, learned and a brilliant talker was conceded by everyone who met him; that he might be a serpent in the Treasurer's garden of ecclesiastical delights – a threat so subtle that Nicholas "almost congratulated our Church upon . . . [the] acquisition"[13] – had yet to emerge. In fact, as Nicholas later admitted, he was totally ignorant of Henley's background and training. Had he known that Henley was at heart a non-conformist, someone who questioned the doctrines of the Church as described in its 39 Articles, he might have been more prepared for what followed. As it was, he was completely taken by surprise, astonished by the way Henley tortured words or, as Nicholas described it, by his need to "blacken . . . the Character" of men whose views differed from his own.[14]

A graduate of the dissenting academy run by Caleb Ashworth of Daventry, England, Henley had spent the years 1766 to 1768 ministering to dissenters in a town near Cambridge, England. In March of 1768 he was accepted as minister of a congregation in London's Crosby Square. A year later, in a gesture of submission that was also meant as a career move, Rev. Henley swore to uphold the English Church's 39 Articles, thereby formally renouncing the status of a non-conformist. On November 11, 1769, seven prominent clergymen and intellectuals personally certified in writing that Samuel Henley was competent to act the part of a professor of moral philosophy. A year later, this adroitly repositioned dissenter was regaling readers of Purdie and Dixon's *Gazette* with his reflections on a House of Burgesses' bill calling for an American Bishopric: he opposed it. Grandly terming the proposed bill a "Usurpation directly repugnant to the Rights of Mankind," Henley predicted that it would "continue the present unhappy Disputes [over the Stamp Act.]" He even suggested that it might "endanger the very Existence of the British Empire in America."[15] In thus inveighing against the bill, Henley showed great insouciance, if not naivete, as he now found himself on the side of local Whigs who viewed the proposal as a form of spiritual tyranny. In fact, most of Henley's battles in the *Gazette* were waged against other local clergymen, especially the Rev. John Camm,* with whom Henley (like Gov. Fauquier before him) promptly lost his temper. As one *Virginia Gazette* correspondent put it, Henley and Camm seemed to "treat . . . one another . . . more like Fish-women in Billingsgate Market than Ministers of a Reformed Christian Church."[16]

Meanwhile, lay supporters of the bill, Robert Carter Nicholas among them, tried to refocus the debate on the bill's primary purpose: to "superintend the Conduct of the Clergy" – an allusion, perhaps, to drunken William and Mary professors lying face down in the streets of Williamsburg.[17] Now, Henley was more offended than ever. Superintend the clergy? Was that not the business of the Church of England, acting through its proper ecclesiastical authority, the Bishop of London?

---

* For an account of the feud between Rev. Camm and Gov. Fauquier, see George T. Morrow II "The Governor Who Loved Virginians" in *The Day They Buried Great Britain* (Williamsburg, 2011).

Admitting the power of the legislature to make such a law and the power of the courts to enforce it, what right did such worldly institutions have to interfere with the regulatory powers of the Church? No, the more he thought about it, the more angry Henley was, and thus, the more offense he gave. But the real problem with Henley's attack on the proposed bill was the license that he gave his pen. Henley liked to argue, and he was especially fond of sarcasm, a dangerous trope for a man of God. Thus, when the bill's sponsors spoke of regulating clerics with "rewards and punishments," Henley was immediately reminded of the example of Jesus Christ who "withheld from his Apostles those incentives to Virtue, RICH LIVINGS, and rewarded them *only* with *empty* Promises of Heaven!"[18] Capitalized indignation and italicized derision were typical of Samuel Henley's style of writing. He threw off italics like sparks, and many of his readers – not just college students – were dazzled. Others, like Nicholas and his friend Col. Richard Bland, a widely respected religious conservative, measured Henley by his words and found them both odious. But was it Henley, writing as "Criticus," who asked "J.H." in Purdie and Dixon's January 23, 1772 *Virginia Gazette*, "If the Apostles were Bishops, pray what was Jesus Christ? *An Archbishop?*" Nicholas was not sure. But if it was not Henley it was most certainly "a Trumpeter of his Fame." Nicholas sought to justify his misgivings: "When Gentleman . . . treat serious Subjects, and exalted Characters, with an unbecoming and indecent Freedom, the Door of Suspicion will burst open."[19] Whether or not Henley had called Christ an archbishop, he was certainly guilty of taking liberties with serious subjects.

But this was the minority view of Henley. The majority, represented by the Speaker, found Henley entertaining; nor did it seem strange when Randolph promoted him from his parlor where he could usually be found descanting smart paradoxes to the ladies over tea and biscuits, to his dinner table for a religious discussion so enthralling Col. Bland said he would rather listen to Rev. Henley "than see a Play."[20] In comparing the clergyman's conversation to a play, Bland had inadvertently hit upon the problem: Henley was too entertaining to be a minister of the Church and too intelligent to be written off as a fool.

Despite what he said later, one suspects Nicholas never really liked Samuel Henley. Be that as it may, he did not voice his objections until March 1, 1772 when Henley gave the sermon opening the spring session of the House of Burgesses. Henley's subject was the Treasurer's new Toleration Bill and its tendency, as Rev. Henley saw it, to lead to the persecution of dissenters. But it was Henley's pompous characterization of himself as an "individual of ability, rectitude and resolution" arisen to "assert the rights of mankind" that seemed to give the greatest offense.[21] For Nicholas, and for many other burgesses, the dissenters' irregular, open-air meetings, many of which were attended by slaves, were an open invitation to insurrection. The Treasurer did not want to persecute dissenters. He wanted to license them. He did not want to prohibit their meetings. He wanted the House of Burgesses to enact "Clauses . . . to prescribe a Method for establishing . . . [the dissenters'] Meeting Houses; and to confine the Teachers to certain Places and Times of Worship." As Nicholas would later put it in a letter in Rind's *Gazette*, "the whole world may judge whether the Inhabitants of this Country are, or whether I myself in particular, am actuated by that Spirit of Persecution which you have more than once so daringly represented."[22]

On March 5, 1772 Rind's *Gazette* printed a defense of Rev. Henley by his colleague Prof. Thomas Gwatkin. Signed "Hoadleianus,"* it predicted that the Treasurer's Toleration Bill would "compel many of the most useful, peaceable members of

* See p.12 of the Preface for the meaning of Gwatkin's *nom de plume*.

the community to *emigrate*."[23] Thinking the letter had been written by Henley, Nicholas promptly denounced him as unfit on the floor of the House. Told of this, Henley let it be known that he shared Hoadleianus' sentiments and deeply resented what he described as the Treasurer's "presumptuous" censure.[24] In the event, Nicholas' Toleration Bill passed the House on March 12 only to die in the Council. Meanwhile, a number of burgesses, having followed the debate in the *Gazette* and hoping to avoid being stigmatized as persecutors, insisted that the bill be printed so that Virginians could judge for themselves.[25]

That quieted everyone – for a while. Then in August, Henley protégé James Madison (a cousin of the future

President) gave the annual Founders' Day oration at the College of William and Mary, an event attended by city officials, judges and members of the Assembly. The topic of his address was "Civil and religious Liberty," a safe-enough-seeming subject in a colony that was moving, albeit rather fitfully, to a more generous definition of religious liberty. As it happened, Madison had little to say about liberty but a great deal about tolerance. It seemed that he had found bigots in Virginia, or as he described them, "open Enemies to Truth, assisted by the Courts applying well-timed Severities . . . [and] excruciating Inquests." The young orator concluded his address with an appeal that sounded as if it came straight from the mouth of Rev. Henley, as it probably did: "Fellow Students . . . We were born to be free," he exclaimed, "Crouch not to the frowns of Bigot-Rage; nor pause a Moment to join the godlike band."[26]

Rev. James Madison
"Crouch not to the
frowns of bigot-rage!"

A burgess and a member of the William and Mary Board of

Visitors, Nicholas was almost certainly in the audience. If so, he was as hot as the sun on the Wren Building's slate roof. Here, in what seemed to be Henley's own words, was clear proof of his corrupting influence. Here, in the guise of the annual Founder's Day speech, was an attack on himself and Virginia's government.

This might not have been so upsetting for Nicholas had it not been that a week before Madison's tirade, Virginians got news of the death in Europe of the current rector of Bruton Parish Church, Rev. James Horrocks. At once, Henley had let it be known that he wanted Horrocks' job. The Bruton flock was feathered as finely as any in Virginia. Its rector enjoyed unimpeded access to the Assembly, the font of clerical preferment in Virginia. One of the first to receive Henley's "canvass" for the position was the Treasurer whose little gasp of astonishment is still audible, more than 250 years later: "I told you candidly [he wrote], and with as much Freedom, as Civility

The Congregation of Bruton Parish Church
"A flock as finely feathered as any in Virginia"

would allow me, that our Sentiments in religious Matters seemed to differ so widely that I could not think myself justifiable to the Parish in complying with your Request. You answered that your Object was Truth, and in Reply, I told you that I hoped mine was so too."[27]

In the event, the Bruton vestry chose Josiah Johnson, Master of William and Mary's Grammar School. It was a good choice: Rev. Johnson was an inspiring preacher and an excellent scholar, a matter of no small importance to a congregation that loved arcane religious discussion. Henley was asked to give the memorial address for Horrocks in the House of Burgesses, a great honor, and with so many important men in the audience, a great career opportunity as well. But instead of delivering the expected eulogy, Henley chose to "expose *Bigotry* under all its forms."[28] Instead of keeping his sermon under 20 minutes like the worldly preachers of northern Virginia, Henley ran on about replacing *"ritual Observances"* with the *"substantial Virtues of a good Life."* Most Virginians were prepared to abide the occasional clerical harangue, as long as it was short, being of the view (as noted by diarist Phillip Fithian) that "pray[e]rs read over in haste, a Sermon seldom under & never over twenty minutes but always made up of sound morality" was not only efficient but a good introduction to the business discussions that were sure to follow church services.[29] Certainly no one, least of all the Treasurer, was prepared to hear church-going *contrasted* with the virtues of a good life.

In March of 1773, Rev. Johnson became ill; on April 4, he died. A few days before his death, Henley again approached the Treasurer to ask for his support for the Bruton rectorship. Far from complying with Henley's request, Nicholas claimed his objections had actually increased. He went on to list them: Henley's view of his oath as "mere form"; his conception of Jesus Christ ("a good man"); and his term for the Trinity "a persona" – which Dr. Johnson, in his *Dictionary*, defined as "an Actor's Mask." Even with that, the Treasurer's "Inclination was to give as little Offence as possible."[30]

It was perhaps a sign of Henley's incorrigible egotism that he remained optimistic despite Nicholas' reaction to his appeal. He had lost to Johnson by just one vote last time, and this time – or so he was told – a number of vestrymen were prepared to vote for him, provided they were counted among the majority. The Speaker let it be known that he was for Henley, as did former mayors Thomas Everard and George Wythe. But the Speaker was not a vestryman, and Wythe and Everard who were, were esteemed less for their judgment in church matters than their plain good sense. This was just fine with Henley, who saw himself as one of the new breed of clergymen modeled after John Jebb (1736–1786) and Edmund Law (1703–1787), Master of Peterhouse College, Cambridge, both friends of Henley, both "pursuer[s] of Truth" and thus, not bigoted by "formal 'Ritual.'"[31] In place of "all Knowledge and *Orthodoxy*," the young cleric wished to interpose "universal

John Jebb
"Not bigoted by formal ritual"

Love." "If this be Heresy, I glory in it!" he told the Treasurer in a June 3, 1773 letter in Purdie and Dixon's *Gazette*.

He meant it ironically. But what kind of a clergyman was ironic about heresy? Nor was Henley's "native energy in the language of the heart" (as he put it) the only issue. As Nicholas said in his letter of May 20, 1773 to the *Gazette*, it was Henley's way of "blackening the Character" of those he disagreed with by using words that were shocking to men of sense.[32] For his part, Henley saw himself as a man of "rectitude and resolution," "branded with infamy." He was no mere cleric but a martyr, a "victim of superstition," true to his ideas even "at the stake." In truth, if words could make Samuel Henley Christ-like, he was. Only his canvass for the rectorship, relying on the rough and tumble tactics of an 18th-Century political campaign, belied the lamb. He appointed a campaign manager, William Russell, the Secretary of the local Masonic lodge. He sent student emissaries, Samuel Shields and James Madison, to collect names of supporters. He then got his friend Rev. Gwatkin to bait the Treasurer into a dispute over Church doctrine in the *Gazette*.[33]

Meanwhile, Henley kept on talking. Much of what he said was in the nature of asides, dropped at the Speaker's or floated in letters to friends. This is not to say that Henley was discreet or that given his notoriety, his words did not get around in the small world of Williamsburg. Nicholas found one letter so shocking that he burned it to ensure it did not fall into other hands.[34] With Henley as its center, the controversy could be expected to ripple throughout all of Virginia. And so it did, with Nicholas, no longer giving as little offence as possible, making sure it got as much of an airing as possible.[35]

The final falling out came at the first meeting of the vestry following Johnson's death. Before going to the meeting, Nicholas put a copy of Henley's *The Distinct Claims of Government and Religion* into his pocket. This was the sermon Henley had preached to the Assembly in 1772. He had since had it printed in England, with a "pompous Dedication" (Nicholas' words) to Dr. Jebb, who had since decided to leave the Church and devote himself full time to religious and political reform. To the "intriguing, self-interested politician . . . gloomy, narrow-hearted bigot" described in Henley's sermon – and Nicholas knew who he was – this was final, conclusive proof of the clergyman's unfitness. With Henley's sermon lying open before him, the Treasurer intended to cite chapter and verse.[36] But the sermon never left his pocket. The vestry, perhaps cowed by the presence of the Speaker, nearly elected Henley rector of Bruton Parish at its first meeting. Nicholas was stunned. After "some few Animadversions," in which he accused Rev. Henley of having broached "Heterdox Opinions" in a conversation with a "Person of undoubted Credit" – a charge Nicholas knew to be nothing less than a charge of heresy calling for the most conclusive evidence – the Treasurer left the church.[37]

The battle joined, the two men now waged war. "An inoffensive, honest tradesman,"[38] Joseph Kidd, was hired by Nicholas to counter Henley's student emissaries and circulate the charge that Henley was a closet Deist who did not believe in the articles of the Church.[39] Rev. William Bracken, no member of the God-like band, but a newly-minted clergyman of solid provenance, was found and encouraged to put himself forward as the non-Henley alternative. Nicholas then left town, too preoccupied with treasury business to do anything more.[40]

A "Magistrate of the City" (the Speaker) then told Henley about Kidd's activities. "[S]hocked at so black a contrivance," Henley promptly went to Kidd's home to expostulate. Skilled though he might be at upholstering chairs for the nobility – the skill that had brought him to America as a member of Botetourt's entourage – Kidd was no match, socially or intellectually, for a university Professor of Moral Philosophy. Confused by the fury of Henley's expostulations, Kidd initially denied the fact – until Henley named the Magistrate in question. At once, Kidd "began to equivocate, at last confessed." Yes, he admitted, the Treasurer was "his authority for what he had said." Yes, he would freely "acknowledge the injustice of the calumny." Before Henley left, Kidd thanked him "more than once . . . for [his] lenity," or so Henley later claimed.[41]

In due course, the following notice appeared in Purdie and Dixon's *Gazette*:[42] "whereas it is publickly reported that I accused the Reverend Mr. Henley of *Deism*, and a disbelief in the *Thirty-Nine Articles of our Church*, I do hereby, out of justice to Mr. *Henley's* Character, declare that I never had Reason to believe that such were his Principles." The notice was signed "Joseph Kidd." Henley was surely pleased. In doing justice to Rev. Henley, Kidd had all but called Nicholas a liar. Just a few days before, Henley had published his own notice in the *Gazette*. It commended Nicholas for his "Professions of Rectitude," but warned that "ingenious minds" would "behold [him] with Pain" if he should transgress his principles. It was a fatuous, disingenuous remark, one that was certain to infuriate Nicholas.[43]

Henley underrated his adversary throughout the dispute. Nicholas did not (as one contributor to the *Gazette* waggishly predicted) "soundly beat" Kidd on his return to the Capitol. Instead, he drafted a clarification for him to sign and had it published in the next issue of the *Gazette*. He then did what any good lawyer would do: he marshaled his evidence and prepared for trial; that is, he wrote to Col. Bland, the person of undoubted credit who had heard Henley express heterodox views on the Trinity, and asked him to put what he had heard in writing, telling him that he intended to put the statement in evidence at the clergyman's upcoming hearing. After some hesitation – Henley had made the comment at the home of the Speaker, who naturally took a dim view of his dinner table conversation becoming the subject of a heresy proceeding – Bland sent back an outline of Henley's explication of a passage in Hebrews 1, leaving it to Nicholas to decide whether to use it or not.[44]

On June 10, two days before Henley's hearing, Bland went up to Williamsburg. He was there, he later said, to see Dr.

Graham, a fashionable travelling oculist, about his eyes. But he also found time to stop by the Treasurer's house on the edge of Market Square. Nicholas greeted him joyfully. Here was a chance to replace a bland affidavit with Bland himself. At once, he asked the colonel to attend Henley's hearing. Bland agreed; not because Nicholas "desired it, but . . . because soon after I arrived in Town, I was informed a mighty storm was gathering against me; that I was charged with betraying private Conversation at a Friend's House; that I had incurred his as well as Mr. Henley's high resentment; and that a *young Gentleman*, and a *young* Lady were to prove that no Conversation like that . . . passed at the Gentleman's House." Knowing what he had heard and being, as he said, "not easily frightened especially when I have Truth to support me," Bland decided to attend Henley's hearing and confront "the impending Storm."[45]

It is possible that Samuel Henley was looking forward to his heresy hearing. A hearing would allow him to portray himself as a latter-day Christ scourged by colonial Romans; a victory, besides gaining him a plum job, would put him in the way of prominence and wealth. For Nicholas, the hearing represented an opportunity to vindicate his tolerance as well as his piety. His feud with Henley had put his character at issue and made his prose style an object of ridicule. He had bored the entire colony with his letters to Henley, gaining for himself the title "Verbositas." His relations with the powerful Speaker, which had been less than amicable since he helped deprive Randolph of the Treasurer's office in 1766, were now threatening to become irreparable. In short, if Henley was nervously optimistic, Nicholas was probably beyond anxious. A trial lawyer himself, he knew better than anyone what can happen to the memories of witnesses under cross-examination. Here, he not only had himself and Col. Bland to think about but his wife, Ann Cary Nicholas, and her sister Molly Ambler, both of whom had agreed to testify about Henley's unorthodox opinions. It would be terrible to lose; worse, it would be the making of Henley at the expense of everything – and everyone – he loved.

The vestry elected to meet before trial, most likely to agree on rules of procedure. There was no precedent for a hearing on the fitness of a candidate for the job of a church rector. Who would be the judge? If the Treasurer prosecuted, who would act as defense counsel? Henley himself? The Speaker? Would witnesses be allowed? If so, could they be cross-examined? The accounts of participants are mostly silent on these questions, but they do hint at a few formalities. A member of the vestry apparently acted as judge, Robert Carter Nicholas prosecuted and Henley talked – a lot. How much of this could be called testimony and whether Henley called any witnesses of his own is unclear. We do know that Henley attempted to cross-examine Molly Ambler and Col. Bland, with disastrous results.[46]

The hearing was held in a sixteen-by-sixteen foot room on the tower's second floor.[47] After so much acrimony, the forced intimacy of the setting must have been hard to bear. Besides Henley, Nicholas, his witnesses and the Speaker, nine members of the vestry attended: George Wythe; John Tazewell (a purchaser of one of Jefferson's law books from the day before); former Mayor Thomas Everard; Benjamin Powell, the "undertaker" who built the church tower; Joseph Hornsby, the owner of extensive acreage in James City County; William Grimes, a prosperous ferry owner; John Prentis, an even more prosperous Williamsburg merchant; William Eaton, a York County clergyman and William Graves, a mill operator who lived near the city on Capitol Landing Road.

It was apparently some time before runners were sent to call the witnesses.[48] When they were all seated, Nicholas took Bland's letter out of his pocket and, perhaps with a flourish, showed it to Rev. Henley. Henley read it, then asked to read it aloud. Nicholas' lawyer's heart must have leapt up. He had expected the clergyman to dispute the charge against him, not become a ventriloquist's dummy for the prosecution's most damning evidence!

Whether Henley inflected the Colonel's letter with his usual histrionic emphasis is beyond knowing. But even the most circumspect of defendants would have found it hard under these circumstances to resist showing disdain for the charges with sarcasm, and Henley was never circumspect. Not done when he was done, Henley then proceeded to instruct the vestry on the issue before them: the letter, he said, did indeed "reflect . . . on my moral character." The Colonel helpfully denied it. Still not satisfied, Henley read the letter again, emphasizing Bland's statement that "I have always considered Mr. Henley as a gentleman of good but not rigid morals, only I think he is too fond of egotisms." As Bland later put it in a letter to the *Gazette*, "I thought the expression 'too fond of egotisms' had given the offence; but I was mistaken, the terms 'not rigid morals' being the criminal words." What happened next was described in such detail by Col. Bland that it can be rendered as dialogue.[49]

"Those words," Henley repeated, "are a reflection on my moral character."

"I intended them rather as a compliment," replied Bland. "By the term 'not rigid' I meant *not stiff, not formal, not precise,* though, in a private letter to a friend I might not attend to the strict import of a particular word. But Sir, every syllable in that letter is TRUTH." (Emphasis in the original.)

Bland then went on to give the vestry "a general account of

the conversation" at Randolph's house, appealing to the Speaker to say whether it was a fair description of what had passed. Randolph, said Bland, "acknowledged it in the general, but said . . . I misunderstood Mr. Henley."

> I then asked [Randolph] if I did not tell Mr. Henley at the time [that] he explained the scriptures as a Socinian [i.e., someone who does not believe in the divinity of Jesus Christ]. He acknowledged I did, but differed from me in opinion upon some of Mr. Henley's expressions. I was positive; they had made a deep impression upon my mind; I had frequently reflected upon them, and remembered them well. [Randolph] then said, he asked me one evening whether I intended to go to the play: My answer was, I would not, but would spend the evening with Mr. Henley, with whom I had rather converse than see a play. I acknowledged I did tell him so; but that this declaration was prior to the conversation then under examination, and was occasioned by a conversation some time before, at . . . [his] house. He then concluded with saying, he thought Mr. Henley proved himself to be an able divine. To this I made no answer, being unwilling to aggravate; but thought very differently, and that Mr. Henley proved himself to be a mere caviler and perverter of the established church, which it was his duty to defend.

According to Bland, Rev. Henley accepted this account, but demurred as to his meaning and intent. "If I did mistake your meaning." Bland replied, "I am sorry for it, but I am certain of the contrary; I am certain you explained the chapter so as to deprive our Savior of his Divinity." In reply, Henley asked to be allowed to explain what he had meant by "divinity." "He obtained leave," Bland noted, adding, "But whether he explained it to the satisfaction of the majority of the vestry, their vote may, I think, determine. But, let this be as it may, I affirm he varied very materially from his former explication."

At this point, Henley might have left well enough alone; might, in fact, still have had the Rector's job. But no, he had to know whether Bland was aware of "anything farther relative to his principles." It was the kind of question lawyers are taught, then as now, never to ask: an open-ended one, to which Henley did not know the answer; one that invited Bland to improvise and embellish. Of course Henley was not a lawyer. Nor was he alert to the fact that the Colonel had allowed himself to be silenced by the Speaker earlier out of an unwillingness to aggravate. The problem with acting as his own counsel – something a good lawyer would never do – was that it undermined Henley's judgment; it blinded him to how he was coming across to his audience.

"I desired him not to ask me any more questions," Bland explained in his letter to the *Gazette*, "I told him I had been drawn into the dispute unexpectedly, and wished to have no farther concern in it."

"Sir, my character is at stake, and I must insist upon an answer," replied Henley.

"Do you really insist upon it?" asked Bland, offended by what he called Henley's "peremptory manner."

"I do."

"Then I do know more of your principles; you hold the doctrine of annihilation, and that the wicked, in the next life, will, by means of their punishment, be totally destroyed, as they had never existed." If Henley made any reply to this, the Colonel could not recall it. The judge then intervened, saying "We have heard enough upon this point. Let us have another witness."

Mrs. Ambler was called. Her evidence, given "with great clearness and perspicuity of manner," according to Bland, concerned a conversation she had had with Henley in which he either claimed "he did not believe Jesus Christ was the Son of God or . . . did not believe in the divinity of Jesus Christ." She was not sure which. And in fact which did not matter. What mattered was Henley's reply to the following, clearly unscripted question from Mrs. Ambler: "How could you [she asked] take Orders in the Church of England and subscribe to her Articles?"

Henley tried to explain. But his explanation quickly became entangled in "ors", "nots", commas and careering clauses: "One of the articles declares, that whatever is not contained in the Scriptures, or may [not] be proved from them, is not to be believed as an article of faith, or necessary to salvation, so that [I have] a right to exercise private judgment, and might with a safe conscience, subscribe to the articles." Stripped of all its qualifications, the bare sense of Henley seemed to be that "One of the articles declares . . .that I have a right to . . . sub-scribe to the articles." At best, this was a tautology; at worst, it reduced his oath to gibberish. Henley – and Henley alone – would decide what was true. Mrs. Ambler was stunned. "Is there really such an article?" she asked. Henley claimed there was, though Bland, in his letter to the *Gazette*, did not hesitate to say that "if the author of the confessional understands the meaning of this article, Mr. Henley mistakes the sense of it." With that, the Colonel left the church, convinced that Henley had no chance to become rector. As he would later say, it was not Henley's heresies that cost him the position; it was his "vir-ulent style."[50]

The hearing continued. Ann Nicholas was called. She was asked, had Henley "said anything of annihilation in the course of your conversation?" She "could not be sure." Before she could explain what she meant by that, Henley interrupted. "I do not deny it to be my opinion . . . that the wicked, after undergoing a certain degree of punishment, will be annihilated."

Nicholas' last proof of Henley's unfitness consisted of an anecdote of the final illness of John Blair Sr., President of the Governor's Council and at one time Acting Governor of the colony. It seemed that Blair had refused to have Henley, then Bruton rector *pro tem*, attend his deathbed. Suavely, the Treasurer claimed that he "did not need to state Blair's reasons"; they could "be supposed" as well as "easily . . . proved." It was a deft stroke. In failing to specify the exact nature of Blair's aversion, Nicholas filled the little room in the tower with dire suppositions. John Blair's standing in the colony, his reputation as a sober, regular (if not entirely punctilious) churchgoer would have counted for a great deal with these men. If John Blair had rejected Henley in his last hour, who were they, with clear proof of the clergyman's heresies lying before them, to bring him into their church as a spiritual guide for all their lives' occasions? Of course, not all of the vestrymen thought this way: George Wythe did not; neither did former Mayor Thomas Everard, Benjamin Powell nor Benjamin Waller, Clerk of General Court. These men would all vote to make Henley rector, undeterred by anecdotes and unperturbed by tortuous explanations. What counted of course was the majority. When the tally was taken, six vestrymen voted "no."

Henley and his supporters then left the church. Rev. Bracken was called in and given the good news. Did he rejoice? Or did he realize that his own hour of trial was just beginning: that rather than accept the decision, Henley would now turn his sarcasm on him, as he had Nicholas? For the now twice-rejected Henley, the joy had quite gone out of martyrdom. Perhaps the Speaker invited him to dinner at his house. Perhaps there, amongst friends, fortified by Randolph's port,

he was able to put on a show of brilliance worthy of his reputation as a one-man play.

Across Palace Green, Nicholas bundled his entourage –
yesterday's snow had not yet melted – into his carriage for the
ride back down Main Street, past the Powder Magazine to his
house. It is unlikely that Henley's hearing drew a crowd; or
that there was much of a reaction to the result. Though this
was a hearing on what Dr. Johnson once called "the most awful
of subjects," heresy, and the role of the clergy in public life, its
immediate effect was limited to only one man.[51] That said,
word of the hearing's outcome would have quickly made the
rounds of Williamsburg. Inside the tower, Nicholas accepted
congratulations as owed to one who had done his duty. He was
normally a cordial man. So were Col. Bland and the Parish
vestry; so was Speaker Randolph. The only virulent person in
the tower of Bruton Church that June 12, 1773 was Samuel
Henley.

Henley remained in Virginia two more years. He spent the
time nursing his anger. In 1774, he apparently let it be known
that some of the Bruton vestrymen had had a change of heart.
At once, "the majority" (i.e., Nicholas) placed a notice in the
Gazette reaffirming their decision. Henley then applied to Rev.
Bracken for the job of Sunday lecturer at Bruton – a job he had
held previously – only to be rejected as a clergyman of doubtful orthodoxy who should never be allowed in the pulpit.

As late as February 17, 1774 Henley was still railing against
Bracken, sarcastically referring to his sermons as "delicious
Syllabubs . . . preferable no doubt to the *Milk of the Word*."[52]
Had he simply it left it at that, he might at least have kept his
reputation as a wordsmith and a wit. But no, the same pen-
chant for loose talk that had caused him to glory in heresy now
drove him to mix his metaphor for Bracken's cloying sermons

with one for beef stew ("stronger olios") – all "compounded like Harlequin's snuff, by pilfering a Pinch out of every Body's [snuff] Box." Bracken's reply (printed in Purdie and Dixon's *Gazette* on 3 March 1774) succeeded by failing to be clever. "What you mean by stronger Olios, I know not [he wrote], having never, I believe, advanced any Thing in the Pulpit that could be blamed by the most cool and rational Hearer." In short, Bracken was willing to concede the charge of plagiarism if he were allowed to have never said anything too stimulating.

For the most part, Bracken was content to leave debating Henley to Nicholas. As before, the Treasurer gave far worse than he got in return. He was specific; he was relentless. He reminded Henley of his oath to the Bishop of London, given at his ordination, to adhere to the Church's 39 articles and "banish and drive away all erroneous and strange doctrines as contrary to God's Word" – this, while repeating the refrain, "I will, the Lord being my helper."[53] The letter is worth quoting at length, if only to show that Nicholas' attack on Henley went beyond mere "carping at words" to include a fierce assault on Henley's excessive reliance on reason:

> Before this ceremony [Henley's ordination] you must have subscribed the Articles of the Church . . .You must likewise have alluded to what was contained in the Articles, when you engaged to 'banish and drive away all erroneous and strange doctrines.' What now is the question that you have labored to establish by these *authorities*, as you are pleased to call them, except that you, and consequently every other minister of our Church, have a right to oppugn* and explain away all or any of her doctrines, if they do not coincide with your private opinions, notwithstanding the most solemn engagements to the contrary . . .

* To oppose, contradict or call into question.

Had you considered the consequence of allowing all our clergy, some perhaps, with but a *moderate share of your profound erudition and great depth in divinity*, to broach and inculcate their own *conjectures* in cases of the last importance, and this, in express contradiction to the Church, whose immediate ministers they are? Should they fall into any material errors, you may not always be at hand to correct them; or can you seriously think it more safe for the generality of men to be influenced by your carping at words and torturing the plainest texts of scripture, than to listen to the Church, by whose wisdom the Articles of our faith were established upon the surest and most sacred foundations? If we admit the authority you assume and set every one at large, what will become of that *uniformity*, that decency of good order, which you undertook to maintain? Instead of this, we should have a mere *Babel of religions* introduced into our Church. But it seems to be enough with you, that 'while men reason it is no matter whether they reason right or wrong; let them but reason; afford us light and in that light let us perish.' Of these positions, your own examples furnishes an ample illustration. (Italics in original.)

To Henley, conjecture was a form of intellectual play. To Nicholas, it was the direct route to confusion and ultimately, to heresy: in short, a Babel of religions. This should have been of interest to Virginia's Whigs, had they been listening. If Nicholas ever turned against the government it would be to *defend* the old order, not to assail it. In fact, Nicholas was no more radical than his friend Lord Botetourt. Like Botetourt, he was a firm believer in the English Church's 39 Articles. Again, like Lord Botetourt, he thought the English Constitution "the best ever made." In fact, for Nicholas, faith and civic polity were a perfect unity. An attack on one touched both. But the reverse was also true: to defend his faith against one infidel was to raise fears of others, traitors to the English Church and the English Constitution being, in his mind, one and the same thing.

Nicholas never quite got over his newspaper feud with Samuel Henley. His once quiet faith was shaken to the core. For the first time since his 1769 letter to Arthur Lee, Nicholas took a long look to see whether the conditions he had set for his continued loyalty still held. What he saw was this: Botetourt the good had been succeeded by Dunmore the bad, and that his much-beloved Church was under attack from within by its own ministers.[54] Meanwhile, Nicholas was being drawn, with help from local Whigs, into the colonies' ongoing dispute with Parliament: in fact, as chairman of Virginia's Committee of Correspondence, he was now at its center.[55]

"The general Voice," reported New Jerseyan Phillip Fithian from his tutor's perch in Virginia's Northern Neck, "is *Boston* . . . You will have heard before the reception of this [letter], that Governor [Dunmore] dissolved the Assembly in this province on their making a resolve to keep the first day of June on which the Act of Parliament [closing the port of Boston] is to take place . . . a solemn fast."[56] The Act Fithian was referring to was the "Boston Port Bill," one of a series of "intolerable acts" designed to punish the residents of the city for their December 16, 1773 Tea Party. What made it a subject of concern in Virginia was not just the unfairness of punishing an entire city for the acts of a few. It was the fear, raised in Arthur Lee's 1768 *Monitor* essays, that this was merely the first in a series of acts by the British designed to divide and conquer America – that what had happened in Boston would now happen in Virginia.

It was cold in Virginia. A May 4 frost had killed the first shoots and, what was worse, the buds on the peach trees that produced the peaches from which the planters made their brandy. But Fithian's own patriotic sap was up. "The people [he wrote on June 1, 1774] agree . . . in general to unite with the people of Boston and the other northern trading Cities . . . and refuse to receive [British] commodities and keep within themselves, their own more valuable commodities." Three days later, Fithian admitted that the outcry in Virginia had little to do with the suffering of the Bostonians and that the unity he had noted earlier now seemed to be fracturing along class lines. "The lower Class of People here are in a tumult on account of Reports from Boston, many of them expect to be press'd & compell'd to go and fight the Britains!" While well-off ship captains like George Dobby calmly awaited "intelligence from the Northward" before going to sea with their tobacco, the *hoi polloi* worried that Boston would become the excuse for making them fight the planters' battles.[57]

The battle for public opinion in Virginia on the eve of the Revolution was turning into a battle for those whose opinions mattered. A call for assistance from Boston on May 13 supplied the occasion and the regular spring session of the House of Burgesses (the session had begun on May 5) supplied a forum: the question before the House was how to peaceably show solidarity with Boston. For Patrick Henry, who had privately told friends he wanted to bring on a conflict as soon as possible, the question was plainly inapposite. For Thomas Jefferson, Richard Henry Lee and Francis Lightfoot Lee, it was a case for practical politics. According to Jefferson, the four men quickly "cooked up" a resolution calling for a Day of Fasting. That they should then ask Robert Carter Nicholas to sponsor it was perhaps predictable. No one in Virginia seemed less likely to support stern measures against the government than Nicholas; thus, no one was better suited to play the part of the onetime loyal supporter of Church and Crown outraged by British tyranny.

Nicholas quickly agreed to support the bill. Even better, he agreed to be its advocate. Happy to add his voice to the general outcry on behalf of Boston, he then joined 89 burgesses at the Raleigh Tavern for the signing of an association, or boycott, protesting Parliament's "determined system . . . [to] reduc[e] the inhabitants of British America to slavery" and calling for a "general congress . . . to deliberate on those general measures which the united interests of America may from time to time require." As Lord Dunmore later put it, Nicholas had gone from "a man of the greatest integrity" to one of government's "greatest enem[ies] . . . a principal promoter of the present disturbances and all the dangerous measures which have been pursued and are pursuing" – all in the space of just six months.[58]

On August 1, delegates to the first Virginia Convention met in the Capitol building in Williamsburg to select delegates for a Congress in Philadelphia. Before they were done, they also adopted the so-called "Fairfax Resolutions," declaring their intention to refuse further imports from Britain, slaves included. As it would happen, Lord Dunmore was away in western Pennsylvania, making war on the Shawnees at the time – an expedition undertaken at the specific request of the Virginians. In his wake he left a void in which British-American relations could be debated with impunity. Before it was over, the summer of 1774 was to witness six "letters", one "plea", several "strictures" and one "summary view," all seeking to advise Virginians on the course to be taken in the upcoming Congress.[59]

Setting aside the more congenial spirit of his 1768 satire of Arthur Lee, *Essay on Pride,** lawyer Thomson Mason led off his

---

* For an account of the feud that inspired Mason's *Essay on Pride*, see George T. Morrow II, *Williamsburg at Dawn* (Williamsburg, 2011).

Letters of the British American with a sobering survey of "the present state of affairs" – a prelude to what he promised would be advice on "what ought to be the conduct of the inhabitants of British America." Six letters later, he was still not sure whether it should be rebellion or submission, and even less sure whether his *Letters* had been a good idea to begin with. Attorney General John Randolph's *Considerations on the Present State of Virginia*, or, as it is now usually termed, *A Plea for Moderation*, argued the loyalist case, but so ineffectually it is still painful to read.[60]

Judged simply as an entreaty or a supplication, Randolph's *Plea* was a disaster. It convinced no one and insulted everyone. What is worse, the insult seemed to be intentional, a response, perhaps, to the daily insults Randolph and his family were receiving from patriotic thugs. (There is some room for sympathy: Randolph was almost certainly put up to the job by Lord Dunmore.) Expressing disdain for any member of the "giddy multitude" who found the government's actions offensive, Randolph proceeded to dismiss most of his audience as irrational:

> My Address is to the Publick. To that Tribunal I apply, as a proper one, to determine the Rectitude of my Sentiments. When I mention the Publick, I mean to include only the rational Part of it. The ignorant Vulgar are as unfit to judge of the Modes, as they are unable to manage the Reins, of Government. I must beg leave to exclude also from my Judicature every Man who possesses not a serene Mind, and sound Understanding. Cool Reasoning seldom influences the Clamorous, but Men of Temper will always hearken to it. To such Judges I appeal; and if what I say be approved of, I hope that those Gentlemen who agree with me in Opinion will have

Resolution enough to avow their Concurrence; but if otherwise, I am open to Conviction, and wish to be enlightened with better Thoughts.[61]

Instead of embracing his audience, Randolph purged it, man by man, until only "Men of Temper" were left. For the cool few who survived his *Plea* as-a-process-of-elimination, the payoff was not a revelation of the truth but the wan hope that they would entertain "better thoughts" and avow them in public.

If *A Plea* is notable now, it is only because it was pressed into service as straight man for what has been called "one of the most devastating tracts published in pre-Revolutionary America": Robert Carter Nicholas' August 1774 *Strictures on the Attorney General's Plea for Moderation*.[62] That Nicholas changed minds with his *Strictures* is easy to imagine. Like his pompous colleague, Nicholas was an officer in His Majesty's government in Virginia; unlike Randolph, who was viewed as a person of doubtful morality even by other loyalists, Nicholas was generally regarded as a man of unimpeachable integrity. Had he not recently given offence to Lord Dunmore with his support for Jefferson's Day of Fasting? Structurally, *Strictures* is an extension of Nicholas' argument against Samuel Henley's carping at words, (and, incidentally, his critique of Henley's overuse of italics), but this time it is for the purpose of ridiculing pomposity;*

That the Author of this *little Performance* was *born in Virginia*, I shall not question, since he has been pleased to tell us the Fact was *really so*. It seems equally immaterial whether the *Principles*, in which he was nurtured, were of a mixed or *simple* Nature, as it must be obvious that *one Kind*

---

* A condensed version of Nicholas' *Strictures*, arguably the most important (and persuasive) of the four essays published in Virginia in the epochal summer of 1774, can be be found in the *Appendix*.

of those *Principles* solely predominates at present and has given his Mind a strange and unaccountable *Bias*. The perfect Enjoyment of his private *Freedom* in thinking for himself and offering his *Sentiments* to this Country upon every Occasion, I wish not to interrupt; but he must excuse me, if I should differ with him in Opinion, as to his being so *devoted a Servant* to the welfare of this Community, as he professes himself. Whether the *Serenity* of my Mind or the *Soundness* of my Understanding will justify me in offering myself a *Candidate* for a Seat in his exclusive Judicature, I will not determine; all I shall engage for is, that I will not be clamorous.[63] (Italics in original).

Passages like this ensured that Nicholas' "detonation" (as one scholar has described *Strictures*) would be audible even in England where Nicholas' friend Arthur Lee was doing his best to get British radical John Wilkes elected Lord Mayor of London. In any case, the restraints Nicholas had placed on himself in his two 1769 letters to Lee were now completely removed. As Robert L. Scribner, without doubt the best editor the Treasurer was to ever have, wrote in 1973,

Now it has historically been found a delicate business to become involved in a quarrel with a saint. For one thing, virtue, unlike vice, is unrestrained by conscience. And with Nicholas, there was that innate kindness, so that once the limits of his compliance were passed, he detonated, which, the evenness of his temper considered, caused everything to go up at once. Randolph was exceedingly ill-advised in having risked such an adversary. His own arguments were dissected and exposed as so much twaddle, and he was rendered an object of ridicule in one of the most devastating tracts published in pre-Revolutionary America. From this exchange the treasurer emerged more than a saint alone: he was a lawyer, the attorney general a pettifogger; he an historian, Randolph a dabbler; he a logician, Randolph a sophist; he a philosopher, Randolph a obscurantist; he a master psychologist, Randolph a hopeless amateur hoist high on his own petard.[64]

What makes *Strictures* so devastating? The fact that it was directed at the Attorney General, a man held in such low esteem that he could be described as "that villain," by other loyalists was one reason.[65] Randolph's friendship with Dunmore was another. But that only raised new questions. Was this about politics or character? And why was Nicholas so angry?

He gave his reasons: because petitions for redress had proved useless; because when "a Sister Colony [was] grievously oppressed by the Hand of Power . . . [he was] surely called upon *loudly* by every Principle of Justice, of public Virtue, and by every Motive to Self Preservation, to pursue such *legal* and *proper* Means, as are most likely to save them from Ruin"; because, though his heart still "glow[ed] with the *purest Sentiments of Duty and Affection*" to King and government he "cannot lose sight of what is due to our Country, ourselves and our Posterity";[66] because John Randolph had implied that the four radical chefs who cooked up the idea of a Day of Fasting had used him; because Randolph's sneering attack on the Day of Fasting was really an attack on religion itself. It is not logic or political conviction that gives *Strictures* its power but anger, the anger of a decent man provoked beyond endurance.

Nicholas' assault on Randolph's *Plea* concedes nothing, except by way of sarcasm: No pleas from old colleagues at the bar – not even moderation itself – are allowed to escape the Treasurer's "silent, contemptuous Indifference," expressed in italics trembling with indignation.[67] In fact, many of Nicholas' arguments are merely *ad hominem* attacks. Randolph's wit is "affected"; his ridicule "despicable"; his doctrines "servile, dangerous."[68] For his adversary's affected modesty (*"this little Performance"*) Nicholas has only contempt.[69] Even Randolph's opposition to the Day of Fasting is cowardly. Why? Because he failed to oppose it openly: "[I] should be glad to know [wrote Nicholas] whether he opened his mouth against it at [the recent Convention]? Surely he could not want that resolution he so earnestly recommends to have avowed his disapprobation."[70]

As for himself, Nicholas was so "affected by the gloomy Prospect" of war that it "hath even *harowed up* [his] *very soul*,"[71] his resort to biblical language being perhaps an indication of the depth and intensity of his anguish. In response to the Attorney General's suggestion that Virginians seek a redress of grievances, Nicholas offered alarm that the government was acting "contrary to every Principle of Law and Justice" and the conviction that its acts were "utterly subversive of everything dear and valuable." In short, the writer of *Strictures* seemed to be a man beside himself; or at least, a man beyond mere strictures. Had Nicholas come around to the views (if not the argumentative style) of his friend Arthur Lee? *He* certainly seemed to think so: he proudly sent a copy of his essay to Lee in London, calling it his answer to "a late very extraordinary exhibition." It seemed that he too had detected a British plot, "Wheels within Wheels, to be put in Motion by secret Springs." So sure was Nicholas that the government intended to punish "constructive Treasons" that even disproof could not dissuade him. So fierce, so brutal that it still surprises some readers, Nicholas' *Strictures* is really a verbal shooting gallery in which its sitting target, Randolph, seems *less* sympathetic for being so passive.[72] Nicholas was forcing people to choose: patriotism and integrity or his adversary's villainous servility.

Laid alongside Randolph's Plea, *Strictures* reads much like a biblical malediction. Nicholas' own view was that it was written to correct "material Errours in . . . Fact; to shew the Futility of the Author's Reasoning" and "vindicate America . . . and our Late House . . . from illiberal and unjust Censures." That might convince some members of Randolph's judicature, who presumably believed that revolutions must have reasons. But surely most of Nicholas' readers saw that his purpose was not to correct Randolph's errors, but to defend everything "dear and valuable" from the moral and poltical evil that he represented.

In Nicholas' view, Randolph was a compromised man. His superior airs, his friendship with the "whoremaster" Dunmore and his bought-and-paid-for *Plea* might all have been cited by the Treasurer in his bill of particulars. But it was the last paragraph, in effect a sentence of exile, which Randolph must have felt most painfully:

That he is determined to act with *Caution*, none, I believe, will doubt; but I have lived to see some very *cautious* Persons fall through their *deepest Schemes*. Could the Author Suppose that those servile, dangerous Doctrines he hath advanced would remain unnoticed? With what Justice or Propriety could he presume to censure what he is pleased to call the *Severity of some Men's Tempers*, when he so roundly charges those, who differ from him in Sentiments, with Want of 'Integrity'; with the 'Arts of *Dissimulation*' and almost every Species of Baseness? Could he flatter himself that '*Men of Sense*' would not see through his 'Deception,' and, as easily, distinguish it from 'Reality,' notwithstanding the solemn Appeal he makes to that *great 'Day, when the Actions of all Men will be fully discovered* and their Integrity known?'[73] (Italics in original.)

It was not Randolph's sneers about the Day of Fasting that

Nicholas found infuriating. It was his "want of 'integrity,'" his hypocrisy – his gall – in charging others with a want of integrity. The point of *Strictures* then was to turn that argument around; to hoist Randolph on the petard of his own hypocrisy; to convict him of "arts of dissimulation and almost every species of baseness." If this looked strikingly similar to Nicholas' war with Henley, it was because it was. Like Henley, Randolph had used "affected wit or ridicule; those very despicable things . . . in a cause of [a] . . . serious and important a nature"; like Henley, Randolph had proved himself corrupt in thought and in action. He too was a heretic. But the orthodoxy he had traduced was not American values; it was the still-revered English predicate for those values, the Botetourtian ideal of deep faith and high principles.

How many Virginians had their minds changed by Nicholas' *Strictures* is unknown. Nicholas' own mind, it seems clear, was not finally and completely changed until 1775. Rhetorical arguments about British slavery and American liberties did not persuade him. Nicholas' grievance was not against Great Britain, let alone his beloved English Church and Constitution. It was against the corrupt stewards of those institutions; it was against immorality and for virtue.

Randolph's idea of America as a store of public virtue was debased by his own lack of character, the same lack of character that, in Nicholas view, caused him to place so little value on private morality:

Public Virtue is what we earnestly wish to rouse and excite in every American Breast; since, without it, we may probably suffer in the very best of Causes. But why is private Virtue so low in his [Randolph's] Esteem? Without this, the other, in my Judgment, is like the Baseless Fabrick of a Vision. If a Man is not just to himself, I can hardly suppose he will be so to others, upon any trying Emergency. What is called public Virtue, unless built on private Virtue, will become too precarious and unstable to be relied on. A Man, with a small Stock of private Virtues, may, indeed, as his Interest governs, do a Thing, from which the Public may reap Advantage; shift but the Scene; let his Interest draw him in a different Direction, and we shall find him, Proteus like, put on a new Livery. It may be relied on as a certain Truth, exemplified by the most extensive Experience, that no Man can be safely trusted, who does not act upon solid, virtuous Principles.[74]

Whether Nicholas' contempt for Randolph had more to do with his morals or his politics is unclear. But we need not doubt whether it was genuine. Nicholas cordially detested Randolph; and his disgust inspired as pure an avowal of his politics of faith, duty and virtue as the Treasurer ever gave. For this, his preferred model was not another American but the quintessential example of English manners and morals, Lord Botetourt.

Jefferson's visit to the Treasurer's parlor on the eve of Henley's June 12, 1773 trial was pure coincidence, his absence from the Virginia Convention and Congress wholly excusable. At the same time, it must be said that his absence was hardly noticed; that though he was a valued presence in the House of Burgesses, he was not so valued as to be chosen one of six delegates to represent Virginia in the 1774 Congress. Perhaps, at the age of 31 he was still too young, too scholarly and too unwilling to raise his voice in debate – a sound Whig, but too untested and diffident to be given precedence over a Patrick Henry or a Richard Henry Lee. He started out from Monticello to go to the Convention in the last days of July 1774 only to have to turn back midway, ironically brought to his knees, the position of prayer, by a volcanic dysentery.[75] In his place, he sent a 50 page scholarly essay, *A Summary View of the Rights of British America*.[76] It came too late to be of much use to the delegates. It was also (in Jefferson's view) "a leap . . . too long as yet for the mass of our citizens." The Speaker had it read (to less than unanimous praise) one evening at his home, then brought it to the House and left it lying on a table for perusal.[77] Jefferson also sent a copy to Patrick Henry who (he said) was "too lazy to read it." Later, a group of the essay's admirers got up a fund to have it published by *Gazette* publisher Clementina Rind. Despite this monetary vote of confidence, Jefferson never got over the neglect of his great leap. (The fact that its popularity in England had more to do with its preface – a fiery call to arms by Arthur Lee – than to the cogency of Jefferson's arguments may have helped to color his thinking.[78])

Summary View did demolish the distinction between internal and external taxation that had proved so helpful as a political half way house for moderates like Benjamin Franklin. But that also was its failing: it offered no model for readers trying to imagine their own apostasy. In fact, Nicholas' *Strictures* were the exact opposite of Jefferson's scholarly "tract for the times."[79] Whereas Jefferson revealed great learning and wrote in "glowing" sentences, Nicholas detonated. While Jefferson was cogently analyzing the pros and cons, Nicholas was expressing anguish at finding his deepest beliefs traduced. Jefferson's *Summary View* deserves its praise; it is an excellent précis of revolutionary ideology. But if the issue is how Virginia in the summer of 1774 crossed over the emotional divide from loyalty to rebellion, the answer is to be found in *Strictures*.

By the fall of 1775, both John Randoph and Rev. Henley had gone into exile in London, to be followed shortly afterwards by their patron and protector, Lord Dunmore. The only Virginian known to have communicated with John Randolph after that date (besides his son and brother) was Jefferson; the only Virginian known to have corresponded with Henley after the Revolution was Jefferson. To Randolph he wrote as an old friend returning Randolph's hope that they might still be friends. With Henley, Jefferson was seeking an address to send money for the books he had purchased from Henley's abandoned library. His friendliness was in the true spirit of the Treasurer's beloved English Church. But in that critical summer of 1774, Jefferson might have done better to ape Nicholas' righteous anger. Had Jefferson known that outrage over Henley's heresies and disgust with Randolph would tip Nicholas toward rebellion, thus completing a process of alienation that had begun with the death of Botetourt, he might have shown more interest in the trial in the tower of Bruton Parish Church that June 11, 1773.

A Scandalous Sequel

And so the story ended, or seemed to. We know that Nicholas remained a firm, if cautious friend of the Revolution and that he died in 1780. We know that John Randolph died, a virtual pauper, in Brompton, England in 1784; that Samuel Henley left Virginia on May 24, 1775; and that Rev. Gwatkin left roughly a month later[80] in HMS *Magdalene*, the same ship that carried Lady Dunmore and her children to England. Lady Dunmore and her children were well provided for. But what became of Gwatkin and Henley? Was there anything in the later life of Rev. Henley in particular that might shed some light on his feud with Nicholas, and was he really a heretic?

The *Magdalene* reached England on the 1st of August. Not long after, Gwatkin was named vicar of Choulsey "by the interest [he said] of the . . . Earl of Dunmore as a kind of compensation for several years superintending the education of [his son] Lord Fincastle."[81] Continuing ill health, the result of being "subjected to a variety of cruel treatment" by self-styled "patriots" in Williamsburg, forced Gwatkin to hire a curate at £40 a year and cease work as vicar. He then retired to Herefordshire (on a £100 a-year pension), to spend the rest of his life as as semi-invalid. He died on October 4, 1800, aged 59, leaving his wife, Jane, and a nine-year-old son, Richard. From the point of view of Virginia's Whigs, Gwatkin's greatest mistake, besides feuding with the Treasurer, was to refuse a request from Richard Henry Lee and Jefferson to "draw up memorials in defense of the congress."[82] Despite that, he was beloved by his students at William and Mary, one of whom wrote in 1773, "if ever the profoundest depth of knowledge and the most extensive philanthropy were united, they are in our Gwatkin."[83] It was a revolution after all – no time to be a loyalist and no time to be a friend of Lord Dunmore. Though his Lordship later presented him with a gold watch, Gwatkin paid dearly for going to Virginia.

Thanks to a letter of recommendation from Gwatkin to his cousin Sir John Hawkins,[84] a lawyer-scholar in need of a researcher, Henley was able to find work on his return to London. Though famously unclubbable himself, Hawkins was a close friend of Dr. Johnson and as a co-founder of the Literary Club, a potential door-opener for Henley with the literati of the age. The fact that "the Knight," as James Boswell called Sir John, had an amiable daughter, Laetitia, may have had something to do with Henley finding the Hawkins home "a place of refreshment."[85] "He was a man of feelings much too warm," Laetitia wrote later, "but this I should pass over, were it not to introduce . . . the . . . suavity of his manners, and the ingratiating modulation of his voice." Laetitia went on to say that Henley had "a taste and talent for elegant poetry" and had showed her some "pretty things," though where Henley's poetry was concerned, "his geese were all swans." The arrival of a young lady to whom the clergyman had been "very seriously attached in Virginia"[86] converged with an offer of the post of tutor (probably procured by Lord Dunmore) to the Duke of Hamilton's two young sons, who were just beginning their educations at Harrow School in London. Within a year, Henley was himself both the father of a son and a widower; in 1780, he remarried.[87] In 1782 the Duke of Hamilton presented him with the living of Rendlesham, a curacy in Suffolk. Rev. Henley's final post, again secured with the help of the Duke of Hamilton, was as the first president of the East India College, a prime training ground for administrators of the British Raj. "I own I was extremely surprised to find him . . . at the head of an institution requiring. . . qualities of temper . . . and a character of mind, diametrically opposite to his," Laetitia Hawkins later said.[88] Henley died on December 29, 1815, aged 70, and is buried beside his second wife in the church at Rendlesham.

Such are the bare facts of Henley's later life. Still to be determined is whether his conduct on his return to England was in a way confirmation of the charges lodged against him by Robert Carter Nicholas.[89] Setting aside his excessive warmth and devotion to elegant poetry (both noted by Laetitia Hawkins), Henley seems to have led a rather simple life. The only sign that he harbored exotic tastes was his interest in oriental art and culture, especially ancient Persian literature, a field in which he was thought to be something of an expert. Bishop Thomas Percy, a member of Dr. Johnson's Club and himself a collector of old ballads, once described "a specimen of [Henley's] Indian oratory . . . [as] a masterpiece of its kind [adding] . . . It is the eloquence of *sentiment*, [*sic*] and penetrates through the soul, – infinitely more forcible than the eloquence of language."[89] In fact, the list of Henley's literary performances is as diverse as it is extensive and includes, besides a scholarly note on a Persian inscription on a rock, three sermons, some observations on Virgil, an essay on certain "Controverted Passages in St. Peter and St. Jude" and three works in which Henley acted as the editor: *Travels Through Spain, 1775 and 1776, Travels in the Two Sicilies*, both by Henry Swinburne, and perhaps most notably, *The History of the Caliph Vathek, from an unpublished Manuscript; with Notes, Critical and Explanatory.* The Swinburne books are particularly fine examples of Grand Tour travel literature, distinguishable from other books of this genre by the author's exceptional good taste and entertaining writing style. In the case of *Vathek*, the original of which was in French, Henley acted as translator and editor. Though a later critic would think it fit to warn *Vathek's* readers that it was "a truly singular work," early readers were only too happy to immerse themselves in the novel's lush landscapes and exotic interiors.[90]

They first had to find it, however. Thanks to Henley's extensive scholarly notes, the text of Vathek is all but buried under the weight of its translator's eloquence of sentiment. The real author of *Vathek* was the immensely wealthy William Beckford,

the then 26-year-old son of the Alderman and later, Lord Mayor of London, William Beckford Sr. (1709–1770), a staunch political ally of William Pitt the elder, and the owner of vast sugar cane plantations in the British West Indies. The younger Beckford had asked his good friend Henley to translate *Vathek* from the French, specifically telling him that he wished its first appearance to be in Paris under his own name. Certainly, Henley had no right to imply that *Vathek* was his own. Yet that is what he did in the preface:

William Beckford (aged 21) "The immensely wealthy William Beckford"

The original of the following story, with some others of a similar kind, collected in the East by a man of letters, was communicated to the Editor above three years ago. The pleasure he received from the perusal of it induced him at the time to translate it. How far the copy may be a just representation, it becomes not him to determine. He presumes, however, to hope that, if the difficulty of accommodating our English idioms to the Arabic, preserving the correspondent tones of a diversified narration, and discriminating the nicer touches of character through the shades of foreign manners, be duly considered, a failure in some points will not preclude him from all claim to indulgence, especially if those images, sentiments, and passions, which, being independent of local peculiarities, may be expressed in every language, shall be found to retain their native energy in our own.[91]

The publication of allegedly ancient texts, anonymous or not, with or without scholarly notes, was a well-established literary convention at the time Henley wrote his preface. Voltaire, in *Candide*, and Dr. Johnson, in *Rasselas*, had both relied on this device to good effect. Nor was it improper, according to this convention, for Henley to invent a provenance for *Vathek*. The case was very different, however, when he implied that *Vathek's* native energies were his own. More questionable still were Henley's references to *Vathek's* author as an *anonymous* "Eastern man of letters" in his February 4, 1787 letter to one "Mr. W," published in the *Gentleman's Magazine*. Not for the first time would Henley ceremoniously reject the "supposition . . . that *Vathek* was composed as a text for the purpose of giving to the public the information contained in the notes."[92] He ought to have admitted that he was not the author. Instead, he spoke of the difficulty of getting the idiom right, coyly adding that since "[*Vathek*] hath passed with Mr. W. for an original, it must have some pretension to favour" and that if W still had misgivings he was welcome to examine the manuscript.[93]

Though a fantasy, *Vathek* bears all the marks of the event that inspired it: Beckford's sexual tryst with 11-year-old Viscount William Courtenay, son of the Duke of Devon. In the novel,

Viscount William Courtenay
"A willing, even eager participant"

Philip James
de Loutherburg
"Asked to create
a spectacle the eye
had not seen"

Beckford is Vathek; his mistress, Louisa Beckford (wife of Beckford's cousin Peter), the priestess Carathis, while the boy Golchenroz is Courtenay, nicknamed "Kitty" by Beckford. Asked to create a spectacle "the eye has not seen," artist Philippe Jacques de Loutherbourg had turned Fonthill into a "Palace of Five senses," complete with something called a "Retreat of Mirth" – Beckford's term, signifying the delights awaiting Kitty in the place of assignation (his bedroom.)[94] The fact that Courtenay appears to have been a willing, even eager participant in this farce was to count for little when rumors of its true nature surfaced; in 1784, Beckford had to leave England. Nor was the presence of Beckford's mistress, her libertine brother George (who brought along *his* mistress, Mrs. Sophia Musters), and de Loutherbourg thought sufficient to dignify the occasion. That was the job of Samuel Henley, who came bringing his two pupils, Alexander and Archibald Hamilton, and their cousins, Augusta and Catherine Murray (the daughters of Lord Dunmore), and stayed for three nights.[95] Whether Henley was present when Beckford led Kitty to his bed-chamber is unclear, though he may have heard about it from his friend, who never tired of recounting the moment to Louisa:

Lady Augusta Murray
"Sufficient to
dignify the
occasion"

Does she [meaning "Kitty"] ever

talk of the hour when, seizing her delicate hand, I led her, bounding like a kid to my chamber? Will she be faithful, will I ever again be happy? Can her accursed relations separate us forever? Is she not mine? Did she not swear she belonged to me?[96]

In her reply, Louisa obligingly recalled orgiastic "iniquities" and "sacrifices," with "young victims panting on the altar" – suggesting that the Fonthill saturnalia involved everyone, not just Kitty.[97] In fact, the others had little choice. Thanks to a three-day snowstorm and de Loutherbourg having shut Fonthill's "doors and windows so strictly . . . that neither common daylight nor commonplace visitors could get in or even peep in," there was nowhere else to go and precious little else to do.[98] Unless Henley was bereft of *his* five senses, he not only knew what was going on at Fonthill, he was part of it.

Louisa Beckford
"Obligingly recalling orgiastic iniquities and sacrifices"

What exactly was the relationship between Henley and William Beckford? The term "friend" clearly does not quite express it. In his own preface to the Paris edition of *Vathek*, published in 1787, Beckford obliquely alluded to the circumstances associated with its earlier publication by Henley, which if known, would be "very interesting" to the public.[99] That we will never know those circumstances is partly owing to the fact that Beckford reclaimed his letters to Henley from Henley's widow, for what was said to be "a large price."[100] Dawson Turner, the nephew of Henley's friend Rev. Richard Turner, later attempted (unsuccessfully) to uncover Henley's connection with Beckford, concluding, "Mr. Nichols is silent respecting it in his

Fonthill Abbey
"The Palace of Five Senses"

Memoir [of Henley], nor do I find any allusion to it in the correspondence ; and yet it must have been very close indeed." Like Col. Bland and the Treasurer before him, Turner found it "impossible for any man to be more amusing and instructive in conversation, or of greater amenity of manner than Dr. Henley." He concluded, "In person, Dr. Henley was short and rather stout; his physiognomy, like his deportment, was peculiarly agreeable." Yet, he added, "All about him impressed you with the idea of a negligent man; and such I believe he was. In the literary world, few of his day excited more expectation or more disappointment. His being placed at [the East India College], I am told, was singularly unfortunate, so incompetent was he to the management . . . [and] discipline of a college." [101]

"Negligent" seems to be a fair description of Henley, encompassing his loose talk about his Savior and his lack of judgment in attending Beckford's louche party at Fonthill. Obviously, he was a bewitching conversationalist, as able to ingratiate himself with nabobs like Col. Bland and Peyton Randolph as with impressionable young men like Dawson Turner. Had he confined himself to the 39 Articles and stood by his oath "to 'banish and drive away all erroneous and strange doctrines,'" Henley might have done very well in Virginia. But he was a clever, questioning man, a dissenter at heart, and it was not long before orthodoxy began to play second fiddle to what Robert Carter Nicholas called a "right to oppugn and explain away all or any of [the Church's] doctrines, if they do not coincide with your private opinions."[102] Nicholas clearly thought that he had detected the odor of sulfur in Henley's manner and conversation – thereby justifying attributions of the sort John Milton assigns to Satan in *Paradise Lost*: a sly, insinuating manner, a delight in the torture of words and a belief in the primacy of reason. Like Milton's Satan, Henley was fascinating – and the center of his own belief system. His presence at, and seeming tolerance for, what went on at Fonthill thus seems entirely in character. Add to that Henley's lifelong delight in attacking anyone who disagreed with him, and it would appear that he achieved his Nicholas-given destiny as a virulent influence on orthodoxies of every nature.

Had he been asked why he voted for independence, Nicholas might have said, "I had little choice. Men like Rev. Henley and John Randolph profaned everything I believed in." Nicholas' attack on Randolph was driven by inside knowledge of the man's moral character, found expression in sarcasm and reached its natural limit in a devastating parody of his adversary's prose style. Nicholas' objection to Rev. Henley, on the other hand, forced him to confront the issue of revolution personally. He did not wish to desert the English Church and Constitution; he wished to defend and affirm them. It is a view of the American Revolution that gets relatively little airing in standard histories of the period, one that might be called conservative, except that it had very little to do with preserving what was being lost and almost everything to do with protecting cherished *English* traditions from being defiled by the corrupt stewards of those traditions.

To apply the term "evil" to Rev. Henley seems unfair. It is unlikely that he went to Fonthill expecting to participate in an orgy. He went there in the guise of a tutor and a chaperone. A better description of him might be "greedy social climber and clergyman-naif in the grip of libertines," one who may well have told his host that he disapproved, as he evidently did on other occasions.[103] But who would make the better chaperone? A maker of didactic syllabubs or a carper at words? And that was Nicholas' point: revisionist impulses were destroying everything that was good and right in the English Church and Constitution.

So it came to pass that Rev. Bracken found himself in London after the war; that a witness was needed to testify to Samuel Henley's war-related losses; and that thanks largely to Bracken, whose name appears on the record of the hearing, Henley got all the compensation he was asking for. It would be wrong, on the basis of this fact alone, to suggest that Bracken was the better Christian. But who was more likely to forgive and forget? A man who liked to blacken other men's characters or someone who hoped that he had never deviated from the Word? Was the Revolution about more liberty or less? In Revolutionary-era Virginia, Robert Carter Nicholas spoke for those who wanted to preserve the liberties they already had.

Notes

1 "Strictures on the Attorney General's Plea for Moderation by Mr. Treasurer Nicholas, circa 25 August 1774," in Robert L. Scribner, ed., *Revolutionary Virginia: The Road to Independence* (8 vols.; University of Virginia,1973), 1:259–285, 281. "Strictures," as it will hereafter be called, was announced for sale by Purdie and Dixon on 25 August 1774, under the title "Considerations on the Present State of Virginia." To quote Robert L. Scribner, "The author was not named, but Thomas Jefferson, one of those who stopped by the house of the 'grave & religious' treasurer's house on the morning of 24 May . . . identified him," *ibid.*, p. 258.

2 *George Washington Papers at the Library of Congress, 1741–1799: The Diaries of George Washington*, Donald Jackson and Dorothy Twohig, eds., (Virginia University Press; Charlottesville, Virginia, 1978), 3:190; Thomas Jefferson to Thomas Stone, March 16, 1782, *The Papers of Thomas Jefferson*, ed. Julian P. Boyd, et al., (Princeton, N.J., 1950–), 6:168.

3 A political conservative as well as a religious one, Tazewell had recently engaged in an acrimonious newspaper feud with Arthur Lee. For the story of Arthur Lee's tumultuous two years in Williamsburg, see George T. Morrow II, *Williamsburg at Dawn* (Williamsburg, 2011).

4 *The Thomas Jefferson Papers Series 4. Account Books*, Thomas Jefferson 1773, Account Book http://hdl.loc.gov/loc.mss/mtj.mtjbib026464, image 362–363 (accessed 12/14/2010)

5 See Thomas Jefferson to Joseph Priestley, April 9, 1803, *The Writings of Thomas Jefferson*, Albert Ellery Bergh, ed., (20 vols.; Washington, D.C., 1907), 10:374–375.

6 Thomas Jefferson to John Randolph, 25 Aug 1775, *The Thomas Jefferson Papers, Series 1. General Correspondence. 1651–1827*, http://hdl.loc.gov/loc.mss/mtj.mtjbib000114,(accessed 12/14/2010).

7 *The Connexion of the Roman, Saxon, and English Coins, Deduced from*

Observations on the Saxon Weights and Money,(1767) by William Clarke, *Piers Plowman* (ca. 1360–1387), an allegorical narrative poem by William Langland, and *The Hermit of Warkworth* (1771) are just a few of the titles on Jefferson's list of the 59 books he had purchased from Henley's library when the clergyman left Virginia in 1775. *The Hermit of Warkworth* is of some note as it was written by Bishop Thomas Percy, author of the very popular *Reliques of Ancient English Poetry* (1765), and (as noted *infra*) an ardent admirer of Henley's skills as a translator.

8   The offer was made in 1770. Jefferson accepted it, only to decline later. (Nicholas had already given most of his practice to Patrick Henry.)

9   *Documents of the American Revolution, 1770–1783, (Colonial Office Series)*, ed. K.G. Davies (21vols.; Irish University Press; Dublin, Ireland, *c.*1972–c.1981) 5:110. A mere twenty-one months later, Dunmore's opinion had changed radically: "This Treasurer [speaking of Robert Carter Nicholas] holds his office, the emoluments of which are considerable, by the nomination of the Assembly whose favour for sometime past there seems to be no means of securing but by a disposition constantly to oppose government, of which on all occasions Mr. Nicholas manifests himself as one of its greatest enemies, being a principal promoter of the present disturbances and all the dangerous measures, which have been pursued, and are pursuing by the people of this colony." *Ibid.*, 8:269.

10   See Appendix B in George T. Morrow II, *Williamsburg at Dawn* (Williamsburg, 2011) for the complete text of Arthur Lee's *Monitor X*.

11   Robert Carter Nicholas to Arthur Lee, 31 May 1769, *The Lee Family Papers, 1742–1795*, eds. Phillip P. Hoffman and John L. Molyneaux, (University of Virginia, Charlottesville, Va.), Microfilm, Roll One. That Nicholas was feeling so feisty about the British government's treatment of its American brethren may be at least partly owing to the fact that he had just come from the Raleigh Tavern where he had joined 112 other burgesses in signing George Mason's Association for the Non-Importation of British Goods.

12   Robert Carter Nicholas to Arthur Lee, 29 Dec. 1769, *The Lee Family Papers*, Roll One. "You know my Voice is for Peace, when it can be obtain'd on honourable terms & tho' I would stand forth in determin'd Opposition to every Enemy of my country, yet I hope Prudence will restrain me within constitutional Limits. I have always thought that

the People of England, by running into Heats and Riots, began at the wrong end of the dispute; they had certainly better done at first. What they are now engaged in, I mean Petitioning the throne for Redress of Grievances . . . surely might have been brought about by the sensible Part of the Nation. We think ourselves extremely happy here in our Governour; he certainly is a Gentleman of the most enlarged and liberal sentiments; we seem to understand each other perfectly well: he is a very honest man, will do his Duty & we are determined to do what we think ours."

[13] Robert Carter Nicholas to Samuel Henley, *Virginia Gazette* (Purdie and Dixon), 20 May 1773, Supp.

[14] *Ibid.*

[15] *Virginia Gazette* (Purdie and Dixon) 6 Jun.1771. The resolution was signed by both Henley and Thomas Gwatkin. In his May 20, 1773 letter to Henley, published as a supplement to Purdie and Dixon's *Virginia Gazette* of the same date, Nicholas wrote, "Your lugging, Neck and Shoulders, into the Debate, the very odious American Stamp Act, which certainly had no just Analogy to the Episcopate, shewed that you had squared your Declamation by a popular Scale."

[16] *Ibid.*, 4 Jul. 1771. The letter was signed "Martin Luther."

[17] Robert Carter Nicholas to Hoadlieanus, *Virginia Gazette* (Rind), 10 Jun. 1773. As Rhys Isaacs notes in *Transformation of Virginia*, (Chapel Hill, 1982), p. 394, n.18, an Order to prepare a bill "to establish a Jurisdiction for superintending the Conduct of the Clergy, was entered in the Journal of the House of Burgesses on March 27, 1772." The description of William and Mary professors "drunken in the Street" is taken from a conversation between Robert Carter III and Phillip Fithian in *Journal and Letters of Phillip Vickers Fithian, 1773–1774: A Plantation Tutor of the Old Dominion*, Hunter Dickinson Farish, ed., (Charlottesville, Va., 1957), p. 65.

[18] See Robert Carter Nicholas to Samuel Henley, *Virginia Gazette* (Purdie and Dixon), 20 May 1773, Supp.

[19] *Ibid.*

[20] Letter of Col. Richard Bland, *Virginia Gazette* (Purdie and Dixon), 10 Mar. 1774.

[21] Samuel Henley, *The Distinct Claims of Government and Religion, Considered in a Sermon Preached before the Honourable House of Burgesses in Williamsburg, in Virginia, March 1, 1772*, (Cambridge, Mass., 1772).

22 Robert Carter Nicholas "To Hoadleianus," *Virginia Gazette* (Rind), 10 Jun. 1773

23 Italics in original. As Rhys Isaac points out in *The Transformation of Virginia*, (Chapel Hill, 1982) p. 394, fn. 17, only part of Hoadleianus' letter survives. The rest has been reconstructed, mostly from Nicholas's letter to Hoadleianus in Purdie and Dixon's *Virginia Gazette* of 10 Jun. 1773. The confusion of identity, which was exacerbated by the address on the letter (to "A.W.") and Nicholas's reference to a conversation "at my lodgings," added a zany, chaotic element to what was already a very complex set of facts. Nicholas was clearly confused. But who was "A. W.?" Was he Anthony White, a burgess from Hampshire County?

24 See Samuel Henley, *The Distinct Claims of Government and Religion, Considered in a Sermon Preached before the Honourable House of Burgesses in Williamsburg, in Virginia, March 1, 1772*, (Cambridge, Mass., 1772).

25 Robert Carter Nicholas "To Hoadleianus," *Virginia Gazette* (Rind), 10 Jun. 1773.

26 James Madison, *An Oration in Commemoration of the Founders of William and Mary*, (Williamsburg, Va., 1771), pp. 10, 11, 13.

27 Robert Carter Nicholas to Samuel Henley, *Virginia Gazette*, (Purdie and Dixon), 20 May 1773, Supp.

28 *Ibid.*

29 Phillip Fithian to John Peck, 12 Aug. 1774, *Journal of Phillip Vickers Fithian*, p. 167.

30 Robert Carter Nicholas to Samuel Henley, *Virginia Gazette* (Purdie and Dixon), 24 Feb. 1774.

31 For the religious views of Jebb and Law, see Edmund Law, *Considerations on the State of the World with Regard to the Theory of Religion*, (Cambridge, 1745.)

32 See also, Robert Carter Nicholas, *Virginia Gazette* (Purdie and Dixon), 3 Jun. 1773; "To Robert Carter Nicholas, Esquire," *ibid.*

33 See Nicholas' reply to "A Clergyman of the Church of England." *Virginia Gazette* (Purdie and Dixon), 3 Jun. 1773.

34 Robert Carter Nicholas to Samuel Henley, *Virginia Gazette* (Purdie and Dixon), 20 May 1773, Supp.

35 *Ibid.*

36 For more about what Nicholas did with Henley's sermon, see Robert Carter Nicholas to Samuel Henley, *Virginia Gazette* (Purdie and Dixon), 20 May 1773, Supp.

37 *Ibid.*
38 Robert Carter Nicholas to Samuel Henley, *Virginia Gazette* (Purdie and Dixon), 24 Feb. 1774.
39 Samuel Henley "To The Real Associator," *Virginia Gazette* (Dixon and Hunter), 4 Mar. 1775.
40 Not much is known about Bracken, except that he was about 30, English born and bred and safely orthodox. Discovered by the Treasurer in his hour of need, Bracken would prove no better (or worse) than he had to be: an orthodox Anglican with a deferential manner and a taste for alcoholic spirits.
41 Samuel Henley to "The Real Associator," *Virginia Gazette* (Dixon and Hunter), 4 Mar. 1775.
42 *Virginia Gazette*, (Purdie and Dixon) 13 May 1773.
43 Samuel Henley to Robert Carter Nicholas, *Virginia Gazette* (Purdie and Dixon), 13 May 1773.
44 "*Lectum viri, vel legendum esse,*" *Virginia Gazette*, (Pinckney) 23 Mar. 1775; Letter of Richard Bland, *Virginia Gazette*, (Purdie and Dixon), 10 Mar. 1774.
45 *Ibid.*
46 Why Peyton Randolph and George Wythe, Henley's chief supporters and two of the best lawyers in Virginia, failed to assist in his defense is an interesting if not inexplicable mystery. The issue of heresy was as explosive one, perhaps too explosive for a politician. More likely, Henley, with the self confidence born of self righteousness (and ignorance), refused their help.
47 Though, for ease of comprehension, I have styled the proceeding in the tower of Bruton Parish Church as a "trial" or a "hearing," it was in fact more in the nature of a general inquiry into Henley's character.
48 In his March 10, 1774 letter to Purdie and Dixon's *Virginia Gazette*, Col. Bland noted that "Mrs. Nicholas, Mrs. Ambler and myself, were sent for, but the two young persons, I had been told of, did not appear."
49 The dialogue and summation are taken from Col. Bland's letter in the *Virginia Gazette* (Purdie and Dixon), 10 Mar. 1774 and Robert Carter Nicholas' letter to Henley in the *Virginia Gazette* (Purdie and Dixon), 24 Feb. 1774.
50 "Thus [concluded Bland] have I given you a candid and ingenuous [i.e., honest] detail of my conduct, and of the transactions in the vestry, so far as I am acquainted with them. It is long, but Mr. Henley's severe

reflections made this length necessary. As it is with reluctance I appear in public upon this occasion, I assure you I will give no farther trouble, although Mr. Henley should endeavor to provoke me with his most virulent style. But, it seems, he is at length determined to put on some part of the divine armor. I sincerely congratulate him upon this resolution, but beg leave to remind him, that he has forgot some necessary parts of it; that his loins ought to be girt about with truth; that he ought to put on the breastplate of righteousness, and be shod with the preparation of the gospel of Paul. These the Apostle makes necessary parts of the armor of God, and if he will clothe himself with them, as well as with the parts he mentions, and if, when he is investing himself with the sword, he will at the same time invest himself with the meekness and humility of the Spirit, I am persuaded many valuable qualities he possesses, which are now darkened by the pencil of self-adulation and vanity, will shine forth in their proper luster, to the reputation of himself, and improvement of others." *Virginia Gazette* (Purdie and Dixon), 24 Feb. 1774.

51 As Johnson had pointed out in the *Preface* to his *Edition of Shakespear's Plays* (London, 1765), the impulse towards heresy was rooted in the "hope for eminence" and the sense that one had nothing to add to the truth. The result: "heresies of paradox," clever plays on words that featured the speaker's erudition and mental agility rather than his insight.

52 For Bracken's two replies to Henley, see *Virginia Gazette* (Purdie and Dixon), 17 Feb, 1774 and 3 Mar, 1774; for Henley's attacks on Bracken, see *Virginia Gazette* (Purdie and Dixon) 17 and 24 Mar, 1774. Rhys Isaac imagines townspeople "peering through the wooden slats of lowered blinds," "the methods used to canvass signatures" having aroused an "unusual level of interest." Isaac, *The Transformation of Virginia*, p. 209.

53 Robert Carter Nicholas to Samuel Henley, *Virginia Gazette* (Purdie and Dixon), 12 May 1774.

54 Letter from Robert Carter Nicholas to Arthur Lee, May 31, 1769, *The Lee Family Papers*, Microfilm, Roll One.

55 It may seem that Nicholas was the odd man out in a colony of free thinkers and dissenters. In fact, it was Deists and "liberals" like Jefferson, George Wythe and even Peyton Randolph who were the oddities.

56 Letter of Phillip Fithian to Rev. Andrew Hunter, *Journal and Letters of*

Phillip Vickers Fithian, pp. 111–113.

57 *Ibid.*

58 "An Association, Signed by the Members of the late House of Burgesses," *Revolutionary Virginia, The Road to Independence*, Scribner ed., 1:97–98. Earl of Dunmore to Earl of Dartmouth 24 Dec. 1774, *Documents of the American Revolution, 1770 to 1783*, Davies, ed., 8: 269. Dunmore was not alone in regarding the day of fasting as a watershed act of defiance. Phillip V. Fithian reported on May 31 "Evening I asked the Colonel [Robert Carter III] if he proposes to observe the fast, & Sermon tomorrow; he answered that 'No one must go from hence to Church, or observe the Fast at all.,'" for which Fithian called Carter "a courtier." *Journal and Letters of Phillp Vickers Fithian*, p. 111.

59 For a copy of the Fairfax Resolutions, adopted on July 18, 1774 at Alexandria Courthouse, George Washington, Esq., Chairman, see *Revolutionary Virginia*, Scribner, ed., 1:127–133.

60 *Virginia Gazette*, (Rind), 16 Jun. 1774, 7 Jul. 1774, 17 Jul. 1774, and 28 Jul. 1774; John Randolph, *A Plea for Moderation*, (originally printed in *Virginia Gazette* [Purdie and Dixon], circa July, 1774), reprinted in *Revolutionary Virginia*, Scribner, ed., 1:206–218.

61 Randolph, *A Plea for Moderation*, *Revolutionary Virginia*, Scribner, ed., 1:206.

62 See Editor's Introduction to Nicholas's *Strictures*, *Revolutionary Virginia*, Scribner, ed., 1: 258 1:258.

63 *Ibid.*, 1:259.

64 Robert L. Scribner, Editorial note. *Ibid.*, 1: 258.

65 James Parker to Charles Steuart, 19 May 1773, *Charles Steuart Papers*, National Library of Scotland, MS 5028, ff. 73–71.

66 Nicholas' *Strictures*, *Revolutionary Virginia*, Scribner, ed., 1:271, 260.

67 *Ibid.*, 1:284.

68 *Ibid.*

69 *Ibid.*, 1:259

70 *Ibid.*, 1:283.

71 *Ibid.*, 1:260.

72 *Ibid.*, 1:260, 261, 263, 268.

73 *Ibid.*, 1:284.

74 *Ibid.*, 281.

75 See Dumas Malone, *Jefferson The Virginian*, (New York, 1948), pp. 180–181.

76 Thomas Jefferson's *Summary View* can be found in most editions of his collected writings. Perhaps the best edited, if not the most authentic version (though it fails to include Jefferson's later corrections) is to be found in *Revolutionary Virginia*, Scribner, ed., 1:243–256.

77 See Edmund Randolph, *History of Virginia*, Arthur H. Shaffer, ed., (Charlottesville, 1970), p. 205, for Speaker Randolph's somewhat cavalier treatment of *Summary View*.

78 Ford, ed., *Works of Thomas Jefferson*, 1:14–15. Jefferson's biographer, Dumas Malone, noted the "inaccuracies" and "intemperance" of *Summary View*, but sought to redeem it on grounds of its "prophetic quality" and its "command of the deeply respectful attention of historians." Malone, *Jefferson The Virginian*, p. 182.

79 *Ibid.*

80 He actually left on June 29.

81 E. Alfred Jones, "Two Professors of William and Mary College," *The William and Mary Quarterly*, (Apr. 1918), 26: 221–231, 223–224, quoting from Gwatkin's affidavit filed in support of his claim for compensation for losses suffered during the war. He was awarded £300.

82 *Ibid.*, quoted on p. 222.

83 *Ibid.*

84 Thomas Gwatkin V (1741–1800) was the great-grandson of Thomas Gwatkin II who, upon the death of his first wife, Margaret, remarried and had three daughters, one of whom, Elizabeth, born 1686, was the mother of Sir John Hawkins.

85 Letitia-Matilda Hawkins, *Memoirs, Anecdotes, Facts and Opinions Collected and Presented by Laetitia-Matilda Hawkins*, (2 vols.; London, 1824), 1:307,310–311.

86 *Ibid.* The young lady was the daughter of Rev. John Watson, a Virginia loyalist.

87 His second wife was Susan Figgins, daughter of Thomas Figgins, Esq. of Chippenham, Wiltshire.

88 Hawkins, *Memoirs*, p. 312.

89 Bishop Percy to Rev. Mr. Henley, 1 Feb. 1775, *Proceedings of the Massachusetts Historical Society, 1876–1877* (Boston, 1878), p. 239.

90 Judge Chamberlin, "Sketch of the Life of the Rev. Samuel Henley, D.D., Professor of Moral Philosophy in William and Mary College, Virginia, 1770–1775," *Proceedings of the Massachusetts Historical Society, 1876–1877*, p. 240.

91 "Preface to the First English Edition," *The History of the Caliph Vathek by William Beckford, Esq., Printed Verbatim from the First Edition with the Original Prefaces and Notes, by Samuel Henley*, (London, 1868.)

92 Samuel Henley to Mr. Gentleman, 4 Feb. 1787, Nicols, *Illustrations of the Literary History of the Eighteenth Century*, (3 vols.; London, 1848) 3:764.

93 *Ibid.* The "sportive remark" that occasioned Henley's equally sportive reply can be found in the *Gentleman's Magazine*, 57:764. "Mr. W" was the Rev. Stephen Weston.

94 Iain McCalman, "The Virtual Infernal: Phillipe de Loutherbourg, William Beckford and the Spectacle of the Sublime," *Romanticism on the Net, Romantic Spectacle*, John Halliwell and Ian Haywood, eds., 46 (Universite de Montreal, 2007), http://www.erudit.org/ revue/ron/2007/ v/n46/016129ar.html (accessed 4/9/2008.)

95 The relationship between Lord Dunmore and the 9th Duke of Hamilton was very close, being founded upon the marriage of Dunmore's oldest son, Lord Fincastle, to Susan, daughter of the Duke and sister of Henley's charges, Alexander and Archibald Hamilton. Of some additional interest is the fact that Alexander Hamilton later married Beckford's daughter Susan Euphemia.

96 Quoted in Timothy Mowl, *William Beckford: Composing for Mozart*, (London, 1998) p. 111.

97 Quoted in Andre Parreaux, *William Beckford, Auteur de Vathek, 1760–1844. Etude de la Creation Litteraire.* (Paris, 1960), p. 382.

98 Quoted in McCalman, "The Virtual Infernal."

99 "Preface to the Third French Edition," 1 Juin 1815, *The History of the Caliph Vathek by William Beckford, Esq., Printed Verbatim from the First Edition with the Original Prefaces and Notes, by Henley*, (London, 1868.)

100 Chamberlin, "Sketch of the Life of the Rev. Samuel Henley, D.D.," *Proceedings of the Massachusetts Historical Society, 1876–1877*, pp. 236, 240 fns. The price was £25, no small amount for Henley's widow, but hardly a drop in the bucket for someone as wealthy as William Beckford.

101 *Ibid.*, p. 236.

102 Robert Carter Nicholas to "A Clergyman of the Church of England," *Virginia Gazette* (Purdie and Dixon), 13 Jun. 1773.

103 In the only letter from Henley to Beckford to have surfaced in the 200 years since his purchase of his correspondence from Henley's widow, Beckford states, "[A]t present I am as perfectly a sober personage as,

to do you justice, you professed I should be." William Beckford to the Rev. Mr. Henley, 12 Aug. 1782, *Proceedings of the Massachusetts Historical Society, 1876–1877*, p. 240.

Appendix

Robert Carter Nicholas' Strictures on Randolph's Plea For Moderation

That the Author of the *little Performance* was *born* in *Virginia* I shall not question, since he has been pleased to tell us the Fact was *really* so. It seems equally immaterial whether the *Principles*, in which he was nurtured, were of a mixed or *simple* Nature, as it must be obvious that *one Kind* of those *Principles* solely predominates at present and has given his Mind a strange and unaccountable *Bias*. The perfect Enjoyment of his private *Freedom* in thinking for himself, and offering his *Sentiments* to this Country upon every Occasion, I wish not to interrupt; but he must excuse me, if I should differ with him in Opinion, as to his being so *devoted a Servant* to the Welfare of this Community, as he professes himself. Whether the *Serenity* of my Mind or the *Soundness of* my Understanding will justify me in offering myself a *Candidate* for a *Seat* in his *exclusive Judicature*, I will not determine; all I shall engage for is, that I will not be *clamorous*. The present distressed Situation of Virginia is what all good Men must heartily lament; but I hope he does not mean to insinuate that we have *wantonly* drawn any of these Misfortunes on ourselves. He should recollect his Latin Adage, *Jus suum cuique tribuere* ["Justice allots to each his own"], that *Foundation of social Duties*, to which, without Doubt, he hath religiously conformed in every Instance. Popular Odium, the Weight of which he is so very sensible of, it is far from my Intention to excite against him; but I am more strongly impelled to dispute his great *Indifference* about an Office, "should he possess one," so very precarious in its

Tenure. My sole View is to put my Country- men a little more on their Guard, and to remove, if I can, those unfavourable Impressions, he has laboured to make on the Minds of *others.*

If some Men have unwarrantably and unjustly, in the Author's Opinion, assumed to themselves that "most exalted and honourable Appellation" of a PATRIOT, perhaps there may be found, in the World, other *Characters* equally exceptionable. I do not wish to limit his Ardour and the Overflowings of his Zeal for the Good of his Country; but would gladly be informed to what Purpose, on the present Occasion, the Public is entertained with so many *trite* Observations on the Nature of the British Constitution; I presume to give them this Name, because they have been so repeatedly rung in our Ears, that the merest *Sciolist,* the veriest Smatterer in Politicks must long since have had them all by Rote. It is devoutly to be wished that the Constitution of this Country were assimilated in every essential Point to that of Great Britain; I mean so long as this can be maintained upon its just, original Principles. Our Constitution, however, such as it is, hath suffered no *internal* Violation, that I know of. Infringements of this Sort seem peculiar to *another Meridian;* had they gained Ground amongst us, perhaps we might not have been left entirely without an Apology, considering the *Force of Example,* and this held out by those, who affect to be so much our Superiors. If the *uncontroulable* and *unlimited Power* claimed by PARLIAMENT over the Colonies is disputed on *legal* and *Constitutional Principles,* this surely is exceedingly wide of what the Author would insinuate. That the Prerogative of the King, "exists here in its fullest *Lustre* and *Vigour,"* and that it ever ought to do so, is what we chearfully acknowledge and earnestly contend for; but the plain Inference which the Author would have drawn from his Observations, if he intends, any Thing *material,* is that, by disputing the Power of *Parliament,* we draw into Question the PREROGATIVE of our most gracious *Sovereign*; than which, nothing can be more contrary to the Sentiments and Wishes of all America.

It seems that every One, who doth not adopt the Author's Principles, is to be considered as a *designing Man* and must no longer expect to be honoured with any Share of his *Confidence*. *Hard and cruel Fate!* but we must endeavour to bear up under it, as well as we can.

That the unhappy Dispute, now subsisting between Great Britain and the Colonies, is of a very interesting Nature must be acknowledged by every Well-wisher to either Country. Viewing it in its extensive dangerous Consequences, I believe few have been more affected by the gloomy Prospect than myself; it hath even *harrowed up my very Soul.* The Reflection that we live in a State of Discord with our Fellow Subjects. whom we formerly considered and still wish to esteem as our dearest Friends; and, above all the Horrors, which every American must feel from an Apprehension that the Mind of his gracious Sovereign may have been impressed with Ideas of a Disrespect and Want of Loyalty in his Subjects, must be extremely afflicting. I will venture to express it as my firm and stedfast Belief that there can be found in no Part of his Majesty's Dominions a warmer and more cordial Attachment to his sacred Person and Government, than prevails throughout the Continent of America; for myself I will speak with still greater Confidence and say that, had I a Window in my Breast, and his Majesty could deign to look into it, he would there see a Heart glowing with the *purest Sentiments of Duty and Affection.* Oppressed, however, as we are by so weighty a Burthen, we nevertheless ought not we cannot lose Sight of what is due to our Country, ourselves, and our Posterity.

* * *

When my *Neighbour's House* is on fire, it highly behooves me to look *to my own.* When the rest of America sees a Sister Colony grievously oppressed by the Hand of Power, and this, for making a Stand against the Infringements and Violations of American Rights; they are surely called upon *loudly* by every Principle of Justice, of public Virtue and by every Motive to Self Preservation, to pursue such *legal* and *proper* Means, as are most likely to save them from Ruin. Would not all the Colonies have the greatest Reason to fear, if they continue supine and indifferent to the Proceedings against Boston, that they might all, in Time, upon a refusal to submit to any Act of Parliament, however oppressive, be exposed to the same rigorous Treatment? And have we not too many Proofs that a regular System has been formed to bow down the Neck of America to the *Feet* of the *Minister?* Humiliating, dreadful Thought!

"That the Bostonians have acted unwarrantably, in the Opinion of our Author, cannot be denied by the most zealous American." He should not be too precipitate in pronouncing the Sentiments of others. Many judicious, upright Men, who, I believe, are now fully convinced, had their Doubts, at first, upon this Point; they suspended their Judgments, till they could be satisfied of the Motives, which actuated the Bostonians, and of the Evidence, they might have to produce of what Part the Ministry took in this Business at the Beginning of it. Granting, however, for a Moment, that the People of Boston might have acted unwarrantably; yet, what hath the Parliament done? Or rather, what hath it not done? It is much to be suspected that the Author, as well as many others, in considering this *mixed* Question, has attended only to one Side of it. Upon the above *Concession*, then, some of the Men of Boston and in its Neighbourhood have acted unwarrantably in destroying the Property of the East India Company. In this Town live a great many Thousand Inhabitants, amongst whom are, probably, many Widows and Orphans deeply interested in the Trade of the Place, its Wharfs, Storehouses and other Appendages. Several principal Proprietors might have been absent, when the

Fact was committed. Many of these must be presumed entirely innocent; the Guilty however deserve Punishment. The Law is open to the Injured; and, if the Agressors can be found out, there is a proper Jurisdiction to award such Punishment, as the Law hath prescribed. From a *groundless* Apprehension (I take the Liberty of calling it so, till the contrary is proved) that Justice will not be impartially administered, the Ministry take the Matter Up and lay it before Parliament. A Bill is brought in; the Parties accused, contrary to every Rule of Justice, are condemned without being sited to answer what is laid to their Charge; a few of their Friends, who happened to be on the Spot, are refused to be heard, and an Act of Parliament, inflicting the severest Penalties, is passed with unusual Precipitation; a Fleet and an Armament are hurried across the Atlantick with the utmost Rapidity, as if it was intended that they should be the first Bearers of the fatal Tidings, and the dreadful Announcers of the Doom of these unhappy People. So much for the Method of Proceeding. Let us attend a little more particularly to the Act itself and its mischievous Consequences.

In the Author's pompous Display of the Beauties of the British Constitution and the Laws of Parliament, he should have recollected one very essential Point more, which seems to crown the Whole, and without which, the Power of Parliament would become odious to every Man of free and liberal Sentiments. What I allude to will be best explained by the following Observations.

To the Parliament it, of Right, belongs to make and enact Laws for the better Government of all *properly within its Jurisdiction;* for the Encouragement of those, who do well and the Punishment of all Transgressors. If Offences should arise, not guarded against by Law, this Defect of Provision is to be ascribed either to the Neglect of the Legislature, or to the Imbecillity and short-sightedness of human Nature. Every

Instance of this Sort should point out to the Lawgiver a *future* Remedy, which ought to be provided with all Expedition and without *Respect of Persons*. When general Regulations and Laws are established, by which every Individual in Society is to be bound and governed, such Laws are *equal;* the Legislature acts upon truly political and constitutional Principles, uninfluenced by Partiality, *Resentment* or the Temper of the Times. Of such Laws, as these, or rather, the *Mode of enacting them*, none can with Reason complain. But we should be careful never to lose Sight of the material Difference between the *legislative*, the *judicial*, and *executive* Pans of our Constitution; since, upon a due Attention to and Observance of these Distinctions, the Preservation of the Whole so very materially depends. Occurrences prejudicial to Society may happen, which have not yet been provided against by any Law; but these cannot be punished, without a gross Infringement of the vital Principles of the British Constitution, and a direct Oppugnation to a superior Authority; by which we are taught, *that, where there is no Law, there can be no Transgression*. We know very well that, by the most just and invariable Rules of judging, penal Laws are to be construed *strictly;* so that no One accused can be subjected to a Penalty, unless he falls expressly within it. Upon what is this Rule founded? But the Reason and the Principles of eternal Justice (which Legislatures as well as Judges should have imprinted on their Hearts in indelible Characters) that penal Laws ought never to be calculated, like Snares, to catch Men; on the contrary, that no One should be subjected to the Pains of them, unless clearly and fully convicted. Again; we have another Maxim in our Constitution, namely, that it is better many *guilty Persons* should escape Punishment, than that one Innocent should suffer. We know *ten* righteous Persons would *once* have saved a whole City, but this it seems is an *antiquated* Doctrine, extracted from a *strange old History*; and the Reverse is now to take Place in the System of modern Politicks. Let these Observations be applied to the Case in Hand. The Persons actually guilty of the supposed Offences at Boston were subject to *the Penalties*, and *those only*, of the Laws then in Force; if there were no such Laws, I say they were not liable to any Penalty at all. Shew me the Law enacted *proper Authority*, or submitted to by immemorial Usage, declaring that the Port of Boston or any other Town should be blocked up and the Trade, almost, of a whole Country detroyed, even supposing all the Inhabitants of the Town guilty, which is not pretended in the present Case, and I will agree that the Penalty might be legally inflicted. There are many Persons confessed to be grievously oppressed by this Act, who are perfectly innocent. Let a Law enacted by *proper* Authority be produced, which declares that all the Inhabitants of Boston or any other Town, whether innocent or guilty, shall be punished most severely for the Acts of Violence or Intemperance of Individuals committed either in their own Town or its Neighbourhood, and I will kiss the *legal Rod*, and yield up the Argument; but. if no such Law can be produced, I take the Liberty to pronounce that the Boston Port Act, considering it in a Judicial Point of View is *unconstitutional*; that, as an Act of *legislative Power*, it is entirely *ex post facto*, in the most odious Sense of the Words; and that, with Respect to all those especially, who are confessedly innocent, it constitutes a new Crime and inflicts a Punishment, which cannot be justified. Here, I suppose, will be called into the Author's Aid, the Precedents urged on the other Side of the Water. I shall not, for Brevity's Sake, quote them all; but refer my Readers to the rest, with the Answers given to them, contenting myself, with mentioning only two, the most capital.

In the Reign of King Charles the second, when Dr. Lamb was killed by unknown Persons, the City of London was fined; and, in Captain Porteus's Affair, a Fine was set upon the whole

City of Edinburgh. I take the Liberty of referring for an Answer to these Examples, in Part, to what was urged, with much propriety, by a few worthy, patriotic Americans in their Petition against the Boston Port Bill. I give it in their own Words, as I would by no Means mutilate that Part of a Petition, which must for ever endear them to all their Countrymen. "The Case of the King against the City of London, ["] say they, was for a Murder committed within its Walk by its Citizens in open Day. But. even then, *arbitrary* as the Times were, the Trial was public in a Court of Common law; the Party heard and the Law, laid down by the Judges, was, that it was an Offence, at Common Law, to suffer such a Crime to be committed in a walled Town, *Tempore diurno* ["in daytime"], and none of the Offenders to be knows or indicted. The Case of Edinburgh, in which the Parliament interfered, was the Commission of an atrocious Murder within her Gates, and aggravated by an overt Act of High Treason, in executing, against the express Will of the Crown, the King's Laws. They observed that these Cities had, by Charter, the whole executive Power within themselves, so that a Failure of Justice necessarily ensued from their Connivance. In both Cases, however, full *Time* was allowed them to discharge their Duty, and they were heard in their own Defence. But Time was not allowed to the Bostonians, nor were they heard. Boston is not a walled Town, nor is the executive Power in their Hands, but in the Governor's; nor was the Fact committed within it.

These Reasons I should have thought sufficient to discriminate the different Cases; but my Objection is laid still deeper, as I am for reducing Things to their proper Principles. Shew me the Law, *subsisting* at the *Time these Offences* were said to have been committed, imposing Penalties inflicted, and I will agree that such Proceedings, before a *Proper Judicature*, might have been right; otherwise, from the established Principles of the

Constitution, I shall not scruple to declare them arbitrary Exertions of despotick Power. Admit but an *Authority* in Parliament not only to *create new Offences, after* they are supposed to have been committed, but to inflict what Punishments they please for the same, and I would gladly know what will become of that Security for their Properties, their Liberties and Lives, which Englishmen boast of, as derived from the Independence of their Judges and the Permanency of Tenure, by which they enjoy their Offices. Let the Author disprove my Positions, and he will make Room for *constructive Treasons and Felonies*; (a Doctrine long since exploded by all judicious, good Men, as replete with Horror;) he will repeal the famous Statute of Edward the III long ago established by other Acts of Parliament, as a Criterion and Test not to be departed from; and above all, he will prove IRREFRAGABLY that a Man may transgress a Law, which never had Existence. If he should tell me or the Power, or rather *Omnipotence* of Parliament and the Necessities of State, I have to remind him that such a Power is inadmissible, since it contradicts a more transcendent Authority; and that no Exigency of Government can commute for so flagrant a Violation of the first and fundamental Principles of the Constitution and the sacred Laws of Justice. If, in attempting to reason on these Principles, I am drawn back to the State of Nature, where, according to the old Vulgarisms, *Might* was sure to overcome *Right* and, where the *weakest* always *went to the Wall*, I must drop my Pen, and go in Quest of a new Topick

* * *

The *principal, avowed Cause* of the present rigorous Measures against America seems to arise from Jealousy excited an Apprehension that we affect and aim at Independency; and we cannot gain Credit, notwithstanding our explicit and most solemn Assurances of the contrary. For myself, I do protest before God and the World, that the utmost of my Wish is, that Things may return to their old Channel, when we lived a free and happy People. This obtained, I would, with Pleasure, say to each Country, ESTO PERPETUA ["May you endure forever"]. He had before given it as his Opinion that *the Americans might argue til Doomsday*, but that he was afraid they would find the "Parliament *deaf* to their Reasoning and their Eloquence unavailing;" what can he now mean by Abatement of *Rigour* on their Part, and *Relaxation* on ours; unless it is, that America should offer a *Carte blanche*, in Hopes of prevailing with Parliament to desist from Punishment?

* * *

The Minds of many People, especially of their Representatives, were a good Deal agitated, at a former Session upon receiving an Account of the Act of Parliament respecting Rhode Island, and for the Reasons before given. When the Boston Port Act appeared at the last Session, the general Uneasiness, that prevailed must be remembered. Many Expedients were thought of and the Measure proposed was the Result of much Deliberation. Its primary Object I have endeavoured to explain; but there were others of a secondary Nature. So far from designing to inflame, I believe it was expected that the Generality of People would be brought to a *serious* and *proper* Sense of their Danger; the Conduct they ought to hold; and, at the same Time, that it would be a Means of restraining them from Acts of Violence and Intemperance. It was, with much Pleasure, I observed that these Effects were produced. Another good Influence it might have been expected to have, was, that certain GREAT MEN of this Earth might be brought to a proper Sense of that Justice, which is due to all their *Fellow Subjects*, by reminding *them* that there is a *superior Power, even a* GOD IN HEAVEN. to whom they will be one Day accountable for all their Actions. As to the ordinary Service of the Church being only performed on the Occasion;

the late House of Burgesses must think themselves peculiarly unfortunate in falling under the Author's Censure for this. They did not *presume* to desire that any *Additions* should be made to that *sacred Office*, which they knew was properly adapted to every Purpose. They did not wish that any Thing particularly *pointed* or *inflammatory* should fall from the Pulpit. A general Display of the Superintendence of Providence, and the *Influence*, which a thorough *Conviction* and *Remembrance* of *this*, ought to have, together with an implicit Reliance on his Goodness, were the Doctrines, which they desired to have inculcated, leaving the Congregation to their own Reflections in making proper Applications. The People of Boston will have no Reason to suppose that it was our Design to *fob them off, in their unhappy Situation, with Fasting and Prayer.* They will *soon* be informed, if they have not heard it already, how very cordially we sympathise with them in their Distresses, and that we are exerting every Means, in our Power, for their Relief. Should we, indeed, pursue [the Attorney General's] Advice, it would be *fobbing them off* with a *Witness.* The Author, not having professedly entered upon that long agitated *Question*, respecting the *Authority* of Parliament to tax the Colonies, I am very willing to rest the Point upon what *hath* been already written by abler Pens, much to my Satisfaction, and to my thorough Conviction that they have *no such Authority.*

At length he draws to a Conclusion and tells us that he has "spoke pretty much in Generals, but, if called upon, can descend to Particulars." It would have been obliging to the Public, if he had favoured them with any farther *material* Observations; but what can he have left unsaid, that would answer his Purpose? That he is determined to act with *Caution*, none, I believe, will doubt; but I have lived to see some very *cautious* Persons fall through their *deepest Schemes.* Could the Author Suppose that those servile, dangerous Doctrines, he hath advanced, would remain unnoticed? With what Justice or Propriety could he presume to censure what he is pleased to call the *Severity of some Men's Tempers*, when he so roundly charges those, who differ from him in Sentiments, with Want of "Integrity;" with the "Arts of *Dissimulation*" and almost every Species of Baseness? Could he flatter himself that *"Men of Sense"* would not easily see through his "Deception," and, as easily. distinguish it from *"Reality,"* notwithstanding the solemn Appeal he makes to that *great "Day, when the Actions of all Men will be fully discovered,* and their Integrity known?"

It is more than probable that a Reply will be attempted to what I have written. Should it contain any Species of Reasoning, worthy of Consideration, perhaps it may engage my farther Attention; otherwise, I shall indulge a silent, contemptuous Indifference; quite impregnable to every Assault of *affected* Wit or Ridicule: those very *despicable Things*, for which I acknowledge myself to have neither Taste nor Talents, especially in a Cause of so serious and important a Nature.

I *chearfully* accord with the Author's Wishes, that *America* may be restored to "the same Situation, in which it was, when our most gracious Sovereign ascended the Imperial Throne of his Royal Ancestors." It is, farther, my most ardent *Prayer* that all those unhappy Differences, which subsist between *Great Britain* and *America* may speedily subside and be buried in *eternal Oblivion;* that a *perfect Reconciliation, and inviolable Friendship* may be established on the most *permanent Foundations,* and, that both Countries may enjoy the *inexhaustible Sweets of constitutional Freedom* and *Liberty* till *Time* shall be *no more.*

ca. 25 August 1774

George Washington and The Immortal Moment

Yorktown, 1781

Washington returned to Mount Vernon on September 9, 1781. He had not been there since May of 1775. Four months ago, with the cause apparently lost, he must have thought he would never see it again. Now he was on the verge of winning the war. His aide (and later portraitist) Jonathan Trumbull, sketched in words the dinner that Washington laid on at Mount Vernon that afternoon for a party of 70 American and French officers: "A numerous family now present. All accommodated. An elegant seat and situation great appearance of opulence and real exhibitions of hospitality and princely entertainment."

Three days later, the two generals and their staff officers left for Williamsburg. To use his own phrase, Washington rode "on the spur of speed." His dispatch to Gen. Lincoln, admonished him to "Hurry on . . . with your Troops on the wing of Speed," while a P. S. in a note to Lafayette teasingly hoped he would "keep Cornwallis safe . . . until we arrive." Only twenty miles down the road, he was halted by the news that the commander of the French fleet, Adm. de Grasse, was engaged off Cape Charles with an English fleet as large as his own. Unfort-unately, the rider had left before the outcome of the battle, now generally known as the Battle of The Chesapeake was clear! Washington was once again free to think the worst. He ordered the transports coming from Head of Elk to stop; the troops put ashore. He then rode on, but at such a reckless pace that by the time he reached Williamsburg, only his manservant William Lee, the Comte de Rochambeau and two weary aides (out of 70) were still at his side.

Washington entered the city without fanfare, riding past Lafayette's camp at the rear of the College of William and Mary so quickly that the soldiers there were unable to do him the usual honors .

> The French line had just time to form. [wrote St. George Tucker] The continentals had more leisure. He approached without any pomp or parade, attended only by a few horsemen and his own servants. The Comte de Rochambeau and Gen. Hand, with one or two more offi- cers, were with him. I met him as I was endeavoring to get to camp from town in order to parade the brigade; but he had already passed it. To my great surprise he recognized my features and spoke to me immediately after. Never was more joy painted in any countenances than theirs. The Marquis rode up with precipitation, clasped the General in his arms and embraced him with an ardor not easily described.

St. George Tucker elaborated on Lafayette's not-to-be- described ardor: "at this moment, we saw the Marquis, riding in at full speed from the town, and as he approached General Washington, threw his bridle on the horse's neck, opened both his arms as wide as he could reach, and caught the General round his body, hugged him as close as it was possible, and absolutely kissed him from ear to ear once or twice." Despite the undignified nature of his young friend's enthusiasm, Washington seemed to bear it well: his face was said to be "painted" with joy – a reaction very different from his response in 1796 when, to win a bet, his good friend Gouveneur Morris had casually placed a hand on Washington's shoulder and said, "My dear General, how happy I am to see you look so well."

This indecent familiarity elicited the predictable reaction. Washington removed the offending hand, stepped back and glared. (We are told that Morris shrank away in the crowd.)

"The whole army [Tucker continued] and all the town were presently in motion. The General – at the request of the Marquis de St. Simon – rode through the French lines, then visited the Continental line. As he entered the camp the cannon from the park of artillery and from every brigade announced the happy event. His train by this time was much increased; and men, women and children seemed to vie with each other in demonstrations of joy and eagerness to see their beloved countryman." Washington lodged at the home of George Wythe; Rochambeau at the urban plantation of Peyton Randolph, the deceased President of the First Congress. That evening, the Marquis de St. Simon entertained Washington and the officers of both armies: "To add to the happiness of the evening [said an observer] an elegant band of music [the French band] played an introductive part of a French opera, signifying the happiness of the family when blessed with the presence of their father, and their great dependence upon him. About ten o'clock the company rose up, and after mutual congratulations and the greatest expressions of joy, they separated." "We are all alive and so sanguine in our hopes [wrote St. George Tucker] that nothing can be conceived more different than the countenances of the same men at this time and on the first of June . . . Cornwallis may now tremble for his fate, for nothing but some extraordinary interposition of his guardian angels seems capable of saving him and his whole army."

On September 14 Washington finally learned the results of the Battle of The Chesapeake: de Grasse (with help from Adm. de Barras' fleet from Rhode Island) claimed to have captured two British ships and sunk two others in a three-hour battle with a British fleet of 23 ships under Adm. Graves. If he had not won a great victory, de Grasse had at least made one possible.

That afternoon, the officers of both armies paid their respects to the Commander in Chief, who stood in the doorway of the George Wythe house and took each man by the hand. In all directions, said one American officer, troops could be seen "exercising and manouevering" under the direction of "their great military oracle" the so-called "Drillmaster of the American Revolution," Baron von Steuben, who could "always be found waiting [at Market Square] with one or two aides on horseback." Under his guidance, the men went through their evolutions in front of "many officers and spectators": after which each platoon marched by the reviewing stand, saluting the Baron and field officers of the day, as they passed.

On the 17th, de Grasse sent a captured British ship, the *Queen Charlotte,* up the James River to bring Washington and Rochambeau to a war conference aboard his flagship the *Ville de Paris.* Having borne Rochambeau's contempt and Lafayette's ardor, Washington was probably more ready than he otherwise might have been for de Grasse's greeting when he stepped aboard the *Ville de Paris.* "My dear little General!" cried the six-foot-four de Grasse, hugging the six-foot-three Washington. We are told that Washington had to submit to another French kiss. He could well afford it. De Grasse told him what he had come to hear: that he would remain off Hampton for two more weeks. With business out of the way, Washington and Rochambeau then joined de Grasse and his officers for an an elegant dinner served aboard the *Ville de Paris.* Around ten p.m., the two generals and their party boarded the *Queen Charlotte* for the return trip up the James River. Unfortunately, the wind had shifted: it was now blowing directly from the west – downriver and away from Williamsburg. Not until the 22nd (four days after they left the *Ville de Paris*) did Washington and Rochambeau return to Williamsburg. This maddening delay was succeeded by an even more "painful anxiety."

It began with a note from de Grasse saying he was returning to the West Indies. Washington's dictated reply lacked the dashes of his note to Lafayette, but it did not lack for urgency. Anger, barely sublimated in a farrago of likely bad "consequences" tumbled out it of his letter: de Grasse's departure, Washington said, would create "an opening for the succour of York[town] which the enemy wd instantly avail himself of, would frustrate these brilliant prospects, and the consequence would be not only the disgrace and loss of renouncing [the] . . . enterprise . . . but the disbanding perhaps [of] the whole Army." He could not conceal "the painful anxiety" he had been "under . . . since the receipt of [de Grasse's] letter." Finally, de Grasse was told that he would be blamed for the result: "if you shld withdraw . . . no future day can restore us a similar occasion for sinking a decisive blow. Even a momentary absence of the French fleet may expose us to loss of the British."

Unable to plead his case in French, Washington asked Lafayette to deliver the letter. But to Lafayette's surprise, when he met with de Grasse he found the French admiral as little interested in the contents of Washington's letter as he was in leaving Virginia. Instead, the two men talked about biscuits, beds and British spies. It seemed that de Grasse's fears had vanished, or at least laid aside. Lafayette wrote to Washington to say that he *supposed* de Grasse would now stay.

Washington supposed that he would too. As someone who knew better than anyone how fate, duty and honor intersected to create opportunity, he now had all that he needed to achieve an epochal victory.

CONTINUED

Acknowledgements

Dr. Samuel Johnson once said, "It is wonderful how a man will sometimes turn over half a library to make just one book." After ten years of nearly constant work on this series, I find that I have not only turned over half a library, but a good part of my life. New friends have become old ones. Some very good friends who read the essays in this series in their very earliest versions are now gone. Meanwhile, the library – I am speaking of the ever-expanding library of the internet – has only gotten larger.

It is impossible to name everyone who helped make this series, but some I must mention. There would be no series without the love, encouragement and help of my wife, Joan Morrow. But for the welcoming attitude, expert assistance and criticism of two truly fine historians of the period, Rhys Isaac and James Horn, I would still be trying to distinguish the forest from the trees. The encouragement I received from my two chief non professional readers, Joan and Terry Thomas, turned a mere collection of dates, people and events into a study of the character of Williamsburg. Other people who read one or more of the essays and made helpful comments include my 90-year-old aunt Rosemary Bauder, Paul and Joan Wernick, Richard Schumann, Bill Barker, Michael Fincham, Ken and Judith Simmons, Fred Fey, Cary Carson, Jon Kite, Al Louer, Bob Hill and Collen Isaac. I also wish in particular to thank Jon Kite for obtaining the French army dossier of John Skey Eustace and for translating one of Jack Eustace's overwrought pamphlets from the French. Richard Schumann, James Horn and Roger Hudson kindly consented to do prefaces for one of the booklets in this series. Al Louer and Paul Freiling of Colonial Williamsburg arranged for me to see Williamsburg from the roof of the Governor's Palace, a view that put time itself in perspective .

Those who are subscribers to the British quarterly, *Slightly Foxed*, described on its website as "The Real Reader's Quarterly," will recognize some similarities between the booklets in this series and that magazine. The resemblance is no accident. When I saw *Slightly Foxed* for the first time, I immediately realized that it was the perfect model, in size, material and design for what I was looking for. With that in mind, I contacted Andrew Evans at 875 Design, the English book design firm responsible for its appearance, and asked him if would be willing to take on this project. He said, "yes," and it was not long before he and I had assembled a team of people who not only seemed to know what I wanted but were able to give me something I never expected to find: new ideas on the subject matter. I especially want to thank Gail Pirkis, the publisher of *Slightly Foxed*, for recommending Roger Hudson as editor for this series. Roger is not only a highly accomplished writer in his own right, he is truly a writer's editor.

Sadly, the genial spirit who presided over the series, read and commented on virtually every booklet and guided me through its development, died while the series was still in production. I am speaking of Rhys Isaac, the Pulitzer Prize-winning author of what is still the best book ever written on late colonial Virginia, *The Transformation of Virginia*. Rhys' presence at our dinner table will be deeply missed. But he will also be missed from the profession of history, where his exuberant writing style and elegiac approach to the past daily gave the lie to the sour souls who think history is about settling scores.

As I began these Acknowledgments with a quotation from

Samuel Johnson I would like to end with one *about* Johnson. It was spoken by someone who did not know him well, but knew of him very well, William Gerard Hamilton. For me, it is Rhys Isaac's epitaph: " He has made a chasm, which not only nothing can fill up, but which nothing has a tendency to fill up. – Johnson is dead. – Let us go to the next best; – There is no nobody; – no man can be said to put you in mind of Johnson."

About the Author

GEORGE MORROW brings a lifetime of experience to bear on the characters of the people featured in this series. He has been a university instructor, lawyer, general counsel for a *Fortune* 100 company, the CEO of two major health care organizations and a management consultant. He received his academic training in textual analysis and literary theory from Rutgers and Brown Universities. He lives in Williamsburg with his wife, Joan, and two in-your-face Siamese cats, Pete and Pris.

WILLIAMSBURG IN CHARACTER

George Washington
and The Immortal Moment

Yorktown, 1781

Coming August 2011

Williamsburg in Character No. 6

WILLIAMSBURG IN CHARACTER